Voices Left Behind

Personal Journeys Through Loss and Grief

Marilyn Kuperus Gilbert, Ph.D.

Voices Left Behind
Personal Journeys Through Loss and Grief
by Marilyn Kuperus Gilbert, Ph.D.

Copyright © 2012 by Marilyn Kuperus Gilbert, Ph.D.

KSA Media
2750 East Sunshine Street
Springfield, Missouri 65804

ISBN: 9780983260196 (hc)

ISBN: 9780985499624 (e)

Printed in the United States.

First Edition September 2012

Dedicated, with much love, to my sons and their families.

*"We are like tea bags. We don't know our strength
until we get into hot water"*

– Ambassador Bruce Laingen

Story of the Cover

For years, I've retreated from the fast pace of urban life to an old, cedar log cabin in the woods of Northern Michigan. In my cabin, facing the lake, I have struggled with the process of transferring my thoughts, feelings, and words onto paper. So many times I have found myself sitting there, totally frustrated, tossing endless pieces of half written pages into the fireplace.

One afternoon when the clouds were hanging low in the sky, I suddenly swept the piles of paper off the table, walked out the door and wandered down to the lake. There, I untied the rowboat, climbed in and started rowing away from shore. A soft breeze came up, scattering the clouds, and when I reached the middle of the lake, I lifted the oars out of the water and rested them against my knees.

The boat and I were drifting aimlessly, first in one direction, then another. I sat there watching the shore, and then the sky. It was so quiet. How, I wondered, was I ever going to be able to bring "Voices" to life.

It was then I realized the comparison. In our struggles, somehow, eventually we gain the strength to pick up the oars of our lives. We can make our way back to shore and secure our boat. The low lying clouds are dispersing and the sun is about to reappear. We now realize that we can move forward and reclaim our lives.

The cover of <u>Voices Left Behind</u> recalls that special Michigan afternoon.

Foreword

As a medical doctor of 30 years, I can clearly attest to the physical and psychological necessity of the healthy resolution of loss and grief.

Books and other resources about death and dying abound today. <u>Voices Left Behind</u> brings us a different point of view. This book is the real deal!

We learn from Dr. Gilbert's stories that *normal* grief can feel quite *abnormal*.

While the subject matter may seem bleak and gloomy, the tenor of her book is one of hope, resiliency, understanding, comfort, and personal growth.

If you are grieving this will help. If you are helping someone in grief, this will guide you.

Carl M. Karoub, MD
William Beaumont Hospital
Royal Oak, Michigan 48073

Acknowledgments

"We do not see things the way they are, we see things the way we are"

- The Talmud

Thank you to my family, friends and colleagues who continue to inspire me with fresh ideas, and help me create new ways to present them. I so appreciate your helpful feedback and unconditional encouragement as I struggled through the many challenges of <u>Voices Left Behind.</u>

Special thanks also to: Susan Doyle who has been with me on this journey from page one; Carl M. Karoub, MD, who consistently validates the medical need for emotional support following a personal loss; and Reverend Thomas Slowinski who continues to affirm the emotional reality that "Memory is the cradle of love."

I would like to extend my personal gratitude to my editor, Annie Moldafsky, who helped me find my own voice as I wrote and rewrote these very personal stories of loss, grief and recovery. And a warm personal thank you to each of the courageous men, women and children who bravely revisited the death of a loved one and permitted me to share their innermost feelings and fears. They are the very special heroes and heroines of <u>Voices Left Behind.</u>

Table of Contents

CHAPTER ONE

The Beginning

INTRODUCTION

"AFTER OUR LOSS WE FEEL ALONE AND ADRIFT"

"Grief is as natural as crying when you are hurt, sleeping when you are tired, Eating when you are hungry, sneezing when your nose itches. It is nature's way of healing a broken heart"

- Doug Manning

The Voices of Grief

Grief has so many voices. There is the "this can't be happening" voice of a parent who has recently lost a child. And then there is the anguished voice of a husband who daily watches the wife he loves "disappear" into someone he barely recognizes after she's been diagnosed with dementia.

I am deeply aware, both professionally and personally, of the bewilderment, denial, guilt, anger, loneliness, depression and - yes - even relief, that those "left behind" share. It's often hard to accept the reality that when we lose someone we love, it's natural to grieve.

Confronting the death of a loved one is a traumatic, life changing experience. It doesn't really matter whether the "lost" person is a family member, spouse, friend, neighbor or colleague. Nor does it matter how or when the loss occurs. When the reality of death enters our lives, we are all left to struggle with the overwhelming pain of personal loss.

As a psychologist whose practice is focused on helping people deal with life's transitions, I have been both humbled and inspired by the poignant stories my patients have shared with me as they navigate through the challenges of their particular losses. I, too, have stumbled, questioned, mourned and eventually understood the meaning of grief after the untimely deaths of my sister and then each of my parents.

It's sad but so true. What we don't often understand, is that grieving is a process. In our contemporary society the long road from hurt to healing is often ignored, misunderstood, or even dismissed. We question the feelings, anxieties and fears that accompany loss and grief. We may even feel there is something "wrong" with us because we "can't get over it" and we become impatient with the intensity of our feelings and the length of time it takes to heal from grief's pain. Yet loss and grief are now considered part of mainstream mental health care.

Finding our way through personal grief can be a difficult, often lonely, journey. However, it is my hope that <u>Voices Left Behind</u> will help us understand that while loss and grief are inseparable, they are not the enemy. They are a natural part of life. We grieve because we care. Grief is, indeed, a testimony to our ability to love.

The Child asked:

"Why do people have to die?"

The Adult replied:

"To make life important."

(HBO Series, Six Feet Under)

Fine Tuning My Career Choice

"When the student is ready,
The teacher appears"

- Buddhist Wisdom

We take many paths on our journey of life. Each path and each experience opens up another opportunity to learn a new life lesson.

I feel so fortunate because I have learned so much from the people whose stories appear in this section. Beginning with my sister, Sally, who was my heroine, I have been inspired and amazed by the strength and ability people have shown as they face the lonely road of loss. Sally's terminal illness and subsequent death was my first experience with major loss, and it was my grief and love for Sally that guided me to my career as a "grief counselor."

At the very beginning of my new career, I was given another learning assignment. I was asked to make a house call for a Mrs. Simpson whose husband had just died. In a ten minute introductory meeting on Mrs. Simpson's front porch, I learned a significant lesson which would influence my practice as a therapist.

Cindy's traumatic story led me deeper down my learning path. Her baby had died suddenly. In her first therapy session Cindy challenged me.

How could I, someone who had not experienced the death of my own child, possibly understand how she was feeling. How could I help Cindy understand the messages of another mother's grief?

My parents, who died two months apart, taught me a lasting lesson about loss and grief. My Dad, Dean, died first after a long battle with cancer. My Mom, Lois, died suddenly following an auto accident. Each death affected me in a different way.

As I picked up the pieces of my life, I realized grief has many faces.

SALLY

"As her voice was silenced, my own voice began to speak"

My sister, Sally, planted the seeds that sparked my career choice, igniting a passion for my life's work. She was such a gift to me!

Sally was four years older, and to me, was a blue-eyed beauty. She had grace, musical talent and a shyness that was compelling. Sally was my buddy and my hero! Also, she had a great nickname - "Sally" - which was short for "Sara Ann." My name, "Marilyn Jane," always felt long and cumbersome. I wanted something perky like "Lori" or "Mindi." The best I could do for a nickname was shorten it to "Marilyn." Recently, I found a post card she'd written to me from summer camp when we were just kids:

Dear Marilyn Jane,

"I know you miss me lots and lots, cuz I'm your very best friend in the whole wide world! I miss you, too!

Ha ha - 'til I come home you'll have no one to play with!"

Love,
Sara Ann

Sally's death, at age 39, was my first significant experience with the death of a loved one. Her illness and death are forever etched in my mind. This first encounter with loss brought me face to face with the pain of grief and the importance of supporting grieving families during illness, the funeral, and the empty days following the funeral of the death of a loved one.

What in the world is Amyotrophic Lateral Sclerosis (ALS)?

"We're sorry," the doctors told us, "there's no cure. She has ALS, also called Lou Gehrig's Disease. Death from this disease is inevitable. The progression of her disease will strip away her ability to eat, talk, move, and breathe. We can try to keep her comfortable."

My life experience with dying and death had been very limited before this happened. Sally's diagnosis was hard for me to absorb. Initially, instead of helping Sally and our family confront the inevitable, I swirled around in a sea of energetic denial. I focused on finding a cure, even considered taking her to Russia where I'd read about the use of snake venom in the treatment of ALS.

Gradually my denial and fear gave way to the acceptance of this harsh reality. Now I wanted to ask her all the questions in my heart. *Does the feeding tube in your belly hurt? What can I do to help? Are you afraid to die? This is awkward, but do you want to talk about what you'd like to wear when you're buried?*

By the time I found my voice and overcame my fears of speaking freely and honestly with Sally, the illness had progressed through her body, robbing her of the ability to move, eat, or speak. Without words, her beautiful blue eyes became her voice, her only means of communication.

What lessons I learned from Sally! She taught me to speak from my heart, not my head. I stroked her arm, cupped her soft cheeks in my hands, and told her how much I loved her. Her eyes returned the love. I became aware of a new vitality, a new spark in her eyes, as though her spirit was becoming more alive even as her body was dying. This was when I began to appreciate the value of our limited time in life and the infinite opportunities for insight and closeness that only approaching death can offer. She taught me how to use that precious element we call "time," especially when death is eminent.

What happens after the funeral?

It was my grief for Sally, her husband and children, and my parents that guided me into my career in dying, death and life transitions. After Sally's funeral, I wondered — *what now? Is that it?* No more searching for cures, no more caregiving. I was astounded by the emptiness. What could I do with my energy?

Sally died on a chilly afternoon in November, 1976. The concept of grief support was in its infancy in the late 1970's. The social message I perceived was that grief should end when the funeral was over. But now my grief reached new levels. I wasn't sure what to do.

At the time of her death, I was in the final term of my Master's degree program and taking an elective course called 'On Death and Dying — Bringing Death Out Of The Closet.' I'd enrolled in the course for selfish reasons. I wanted to learn how to deal with my fear of Sally's approaching death and my great discomfort with anything to do with dying and death. I thought the course could help me become more 'death friendly.'

Little did I know this college course would forever change my life.

I began to research the concept of family-grief-after-funerals. Except for religious communities, there were few resources. The super highway of the Internet was non-existent. There were no bereavement support groups and few referral agencies. It occurred to me that if I was searching for help with my grief, others must be too. I decided to work toward doing something about this void in mental health services.

My search led me to my Master's project, which I based on the development of a pioneering concept of grief counseling programs to help families after the funeral ends. These programs could be offered through funeral homes or mental health agencies. Through my own experience with grief and loss I recognized the need to fill the void others were also feeling after the death of a loved one.

That was three decades ago. My Masters degree was followed by a Doctoral degree and many years of practice. I'm still enjoying the life -long process of learning and discovery. My professional role as a therapist specializing in life transitions, has brought unlimited, unexpected gifts.

It all began with Sally. Just as my big sister led me in life, so too did she in death. Sally was my teacher and my guide, right up to the end. The lessons she taught me gave me the sensitivity I have used in my practice for many years. I thank her for giving me the direction and insight that have guided me in helping others in their personal journeys through loss and grief.

SALLY

her beauty slipped

before my very eyes

I held her head
I began to cry

a whispered fragrance filled our room

seeped into the air

I touched a tear

felt for breath

fingered fallen hair

waited with her, held her in my arms

where she would always lie

njm

MRS. SIMPSON
"EXPERIENCE IS A GREAT TEACHER"

"The burden of self is lightened when I laugh at myself"

- Rabindranath Tagore

I was beginning my career as a grief counselor; full of theories, education and ideas about how a person should grieve. Included in my new counseling role, was making follow-up house calls to assist families after the funeral.

The funeral director had given me a name, Mrs. Simpson, and asked me to schedule an appointment. I was ready! However, none of my training had prepared me for this first experience. After 30 years, I can still remember it in vivid detail.

It was my first house call. This was long before mapquest and GPS, so to be sure I'd find her house and not be late for our appointment, I'd driven by the address on the previous day. Wearing a crisp navy blue suit and carrying my brief case, I arrived at her door at the appointed time. I rang the bell. Nervously tapping my foot, I looked at my watch to be sure I was on time.

The front door was partially opened by a tall woman, wearing a long silk robe. Using my best grief counselor smile, I introduced myself, reminding her that I was the funeral home counselor and we had an appointment. She held a cigarette in one hand, and in the other, a cocktail glass with a floating olive. She just stood there coldly staring at me.

"Mrs. Simpson," I found my voice, " I'm so sorry about the death of your husband."

Her eyes widened, then she snapped: "Sorry? Why would YOU be sorry?"

I stuttered, "Well, I'm sorry your husband died."

Still standing in the half open doorway, she took a long puff of her cigarette, exhaled and said, "Do I look sorry? You didn't know my husband. Young lady, I am not sorry that my husband died."

Fumbling, I took a step back from the door and mumbled something along the lines of, "Well, thank you for your time. I don't think you need me right now," and backed my way down off her porch.

WHEW!

Thank you, Mrs. Simpson. What a valuable lesson I learned that day. What causes one woman to curl up in a ball of desperation, may inspire another to have a cigarette and a martini! Some people prefer grieving privately, and others need help through the debilitating loss of a loved one.

That was the morning I realized an important lesson: grief is an individual as a person's fingerprints!

CINDY

"UNLESS YOUR CHILD HAS DIED, HOW CAN YOU POSSIBLY KNOW HOW I FEEL?"

*"There is no tragedy like the death of a child.
Things never go back to the way they were"*

- Dwight D. Eisenhower

Cindy huddled into the far corner of the therapy couch. She pulled her legs snugly into her chest, methodically wrapping her winter coat around them, locking her arms around her knees.

She had been staring at me, tears trickling down her cheeks, when slowly she turned to look out the window at the dense forest beyond. Finally, she spoke: "Those trees out there make me sad. The leaves are changing colors and soon they'll die and drop to the ground. Then comes the long winter, and one more season will pass without my baby girl." Cindy paused, then: "Her name is Patty."

Grabbing a handful of tissues from the box on the table, she shivered and tugged at her coat, trying to tighten it more securely around her legs. Although a fire was burning in the fireplace, Cindy was shaking. "I'm always cold," she admitted. "In fact, I'm just a mess."

She blew her nose, looked directly at me, and then the words tumbled out: "It feels like so long since Patty died. It was Sudden Infant Death Syndrome, SIDS. God, how I hate that term-SIDS! I'm worse now than I was when she died! I can't eat. I can't sleep."

Cindy gazed past me, looking out the window, " I'm so depressed. I don't think I can go on. I'm obsessed with what I must've done wrong. She JUST DIED! I went to pick her up from her crib and she was dead. I feel so guilty."

"Why am I here?" she challenged me. "You know, when you are a grieving parent, and I mean even if you're 19 or 90, when your child dies, your life is changed forever. And, I feel as though no one can understand this. So, tell me, Doctor, do you have a child who has died? Because if you don't, how can you possibly know how I feel? I just don't see how you can help me."

I took a deep breath. Then I quietly began to answer her question: "No, I don't have a baby who died of SIDS, and I haven't lost a child to death. Cindy, I don't know exactly how you feel. But I do know other parents whose babies died of SIDS and many other causes, and they have told me what it's like."

"Let me put it this way," I gently leaned toward her, "I don't have magic words, but I've talked with many moms. These are moms of all ages who've lost children for many reasons. We've talked as one mom to another, and I've listened very carefully to what they've said. They are the experts, Cindy, because they've survived their devastating loss. I'd like to share with you what their voices have expressed, what they've said to me, and even more, what they've felt. Maybe their experiences can help you understand that you are not alone in your grief."

Her eyes softened. She was paying attention. Gradually she uncurled her knees from her chest, carefully folded her winter coat, and laid it next to her on the couch. "OK, I'm ready to listen," she said reluctantly. "How can you help me?"

LOIS AND DEAN
"Each parent's death brought a different kind of grief"

"But at my back I always hear.
Time's winged chariot hurrying near;
And yonder all before us lie deserts of vast eternity"

- Andrew Marvell

Our grief can be affected by the way our loved one dies, and whether the death was sudden or the result of long-term illness. I learned about these differences in grief, following the deaths of my sister, Sally at age 39, and many years later the death of my Dad, Dean, and my Mom, Lois. Dad died after a four-year battle with cancer. Two months later Mom died suddenly, as a result of an auto accident. Each death brought a different kind of grief. I realized then that my grief wore different faces.

Face of Grief with Dad — *Acceptance, Dignity and Honor — It's All Good!*

Many years after Sally's death, I found myself confronting the approaching death of another family member, my Dad. During Sally's battle with ALS, I'd already learned the value of anticipatory grief, of not squandering any precious time. So in Dad's struggle with cancer I tried to capture every important moment. In his last months, Dad was confined to a hospital bed in the living room of our family home, where Mom and I cared for him. In those months our house buzzed with activity and love. Dad was privy to crackling fires in the fireplace, honest talks, healthy food, good humor, and feisty cribbage games.

We openly discussed his life and his death. Dad proudly said: "Hey, I've done what I needed to do in my life. If I didn't do it, it wasn't worth doing!" Those conversations were a gift for all of us!

The humor we shared balanced the sadness of the situation. One of our favorite stories was about the day a new financial consultant arranged a home visit to introduce herself to my parents. Mom was busily scurrying around, completing Dad's morning hygiene routine, when the doorbell rang. Unfortunately, for the financial consultant, she came a little early that morning. In fact, she arrived at the exact time the home health aide was scheduled to begin her day.

Dad had just (proudly) filled the beige plastic bedpan. Mom removed his full-bedpan and was en route to the bathroom to empty it, when she heard the doorbell. Assuming it was the home health aide arriving on time, Mom opened the door, and without even looking at the face of the person coming through the door, she placed the full, warm bedpan into the arms of the woman who just rung the bell, and said:

"Well, for heaven's sake, you don't need to ring the bell. You know you're welcome to just come on in. Here, could you please grab Dean's bedpan and empty it? The bathroom is there next to the kitchen. I'll go get his toothbrush. We're expecting the new stockbroker to arrive any minute now."

Into the house walked a tall woman wearing a well-tailored black wool business suit, carrying a copy of the *Wall Street Journal*. Calmly, she took the warm bedpan from Mom, emptied it in the bathroom, washed her hands, and still smiling, came out of the bathroom to introduce herself to my parents as the representative from Merrill-Lynch. My urbane, distinguished parents were aghast when they realized what had just occurred. At Dad's funeral, that great story was told, with lots of laughter and knowing smiles.

Dad died a peaceful death, nestled in a hospital bed in the warmth of our living room. His funeral, a memorial service, was also held in the same living room. And, as family and friends gathered together, the fire in the fireplace burned brightly. His service included tears and laughter, prayer, music, food, and many "Dean stories." His death was peaceful. Everything felt right!

My Dad's death reminded me of a line from a book I love, West With the Night, by Beryl Markham:

"Denys' death left some lives without design, but they were rebuilt again, as lives and stones are, into other patterns."

Face of Grief with Mom — *"Did I do the right thing?"*

Two months later, I found myself planning a second family memorial funeral. This time for Lois, my mother.

January can be brutal in Michigan. It was on one of those frigid January mornings, that I received a critical phone call. It's strange how we have vivid recall of particular details when we receive 'the emergency phone call.' Some people remember the time of day or even what they were wearing. I remember how the chill of that day cut through me as I heard the words: your mother, icy roads, head-on collision, local hospital emergency room. I rushed through traffic, getting to the hospital in record time. There on a gurney in the emergency room, I found the frail body of my Mom; crushed, bloody, and full of tubes and IV's. She was unconscious.

The physician placed her on life support. Days passed. There was little hope. I sat by her bed for hours, rubbing her arm, talking to her, watching her monitor for "a sign." There was no sign! As her next of kin, it was my responsibility to decide when to remove life support. I was fighting the battle between my heart and my head. Emotionally I wanted her to hang on. Selfishly I didn't want her to leave me too. Dad had died only two months earlier and I wasn't ready to say goodbye to my Mom. However, the doctors told me there was told me there was no hope. I needed to think about letting her go. I couldn't make the decision.

Cemetery for Mangled Metal

The necessary business of her accident kept me from facing the inevitable. There were things I had to do: phone calls, police reports, insurance claims, and going to the salvage lot to clean out what was left of Mom's car. That was the experience I was least prepared for.

Mom's car had been towed to a huge storage lot in an industrial area of town. As I drove into the lot, a surly looking man, holding a clipboard and chewing on a wet cigar ambled through an opening in the rusty gate. He asked my name, crosschecked it with his list on a clipboard, and then pulled the gate open. I inched my car forward. I had to find a row and lot number. There seemed to be no order. I drove up and down look-alike rows staring at cars with no windshields, some cut in half, others turned upside down. Bizarre, twisted shapes of metal surrounded me. At that moment, I wished I could be anywhere but here.

Then there it was, Mom's baby, her silver Mercury Marquis! Mom loved that car. On warm weekends, she enjoyed cleaning and polishing it in the driveway. Most of the time, she and my Dad would drive his "old mustard colored Ford low-rider" to save the miles and preserve the Mercury. And now that Silver Star sat, mangled, fragmented, shoved into a slot, in a dirty salvage lot, on the wrong side of town.

The entire driver's side was smashed in and the driver's side door was missing. The front-end of the car was pushed back toward the passenger side of the car. As hard as I tried to push away the picture of Mom being tossed about like a rag doll, I couldn't prevent the image. For me, it was a never to be forgotten scene.

I opened the passenger door. Small, glittering greenish crystals of windshield glass peppered the seat and dash. Mom's sunglasses and make-up case were on the floor. When I reached down to retrieve them, I saw the blood. It was splattered over the dash, steering wheel, steering column, and on pieces of glass. I wanted to keep a piece of that glass with her blood on it — it was Mom's. At the same time, I also wanted to run away as fast as I could.

I emptied the glove compartment and made a quick search for anything else in the car. As I closed the passenger door, I spied her glimmering silver bobby pin stuck in the dashboard. I left it there, and turning into the wind, I ran back to my car.

Decision Made

Driving back to the hospital, I made my decision. After seeing the devastation of the car and acknowledging the hopelessness of her recovery, I realized my Mom had been through enough. It was time to let her go. Any other choice was purely selfish.

On the day of her death, I gently held her hand as they removed her life support. Even though she could no longer hear, I said: " It's time to say goodbye. I love you, Mom. "

As I had done two months earlier for my Dad, once again I planned a memorial funeral service in our family living room. Both of my parents' services, which were my gifts of love to my parents, were very similar. But this time my grief was different.

Unlike the quality time my Dad and I had enjoyed together in his final months, the suddenness of Mom's accident had left unfinished business. My grief was laced with regret and guilt. It was up to me to do my own grief-work and resolve my issues. What I learned from Mom's death was something so simple, yet so meaningful:

Follow your heart. Don't wait until someone is about to die to tell them that you love them.

CHAPTER TWO

Understanding Grief

A ROADMAP

"WE STRUGGLE TO FIND DIRECTION — TO NAVIGATE OUR WAY"

*"Challenging the meaning of life is the
truest expression of the state of being human"*

- Viktor E. Frankl

What is Grief?

As Doug Manning describes it, "grief is nature's way of healing a broken heart." Yet, we often misunderstand the intensity and duration of the grief process. When we are struggling to get through this life altering experience, it's difficult to realize that resolving such personal loss can actually become the cornerstone to renewed hope and personal growth.

We can all agree on one certainty. As long as man has lived, he has experienced loss. However, today's technology brings another dimension into our interaction with death. We now live in an instant society. Everything is immediate. A crazed gunman opens fire in a crowd, a suicide bomber drives into a shopping center, a hurricane or earthquake destroys a country and, immediately the news travels around the world. If we choose to ingest "news" on a daily basis, we are also exposed to the grief that accompanies the news. It's difficult, if not impossible, to emotionally insulate ourselves against trauma, loss and grief. Sometimes we need help.

Recently, during a group meeting, one man stood up and asked a meaningful question. He said: "I don't get it! People have been dying for as long as they have been living. What's so different today? Why do we suddenly need these 'special grief counselors' to help us deal with death?"

Part of the answer to that question is that we are all susceptible to the traumas resulting from loss and grief. Bereavement and grief are now recognized in medical and mental health diagnostic journals as treatable health conditions.

Getting Through Grief

Sometimes I think of grief as an uncharted experience, a journey with no road signs. Yes, we may find ourselves behaving in ways that seem strange and maybe even a little crazy. And, furthermore, these changes are unpredictable and frustrating. Just when we expect to be feeling better, we feel worse. At times we may move forward one step, only to discover we have moved back two. We become impatient. When will we start feeling better? It's discouraging. How long does it takes to "be the way we used to be?"

Unlike the healing of a broken arm or leg, an injury which we can actually see, the mending of a broken heart is an invisible process. Often, when we encounter a friend who is greiving and suffering from a broken heart, we don't see the visible signs that telegraph their grief. Without realizing it we ignore their pain.

It's important to accept the reality that, just as it takes time to heal from a physical wound, it takes time to heal from the wounds of grief. Six months after her husband's death, Mandy, a young widow, was shocked when she was told, "Oh come on now, you get back out there. You need to remarry and start a family. It's time to move on."

It would have been more comforting for Mandy to hear: "It's OK. Take all the time you need. Your husband just died and this is a tough period. Do whatever it is that will help you through your grief."

How Does Grief Affect Us?

Maneuvering the emotional roller coaster of grief is hard work. We often fail to recognize how much physical and emotional energy it takes to get through "the every day" after a significant loss. Grief requires a personal investment of time and understanding.

Emotional feelings come in a multitude of challenging guises: denial, shock, hyperactivity, lethargy, anger, fear, sadness, regret, guilt, anxiety, depression, and loneliness. "My loneliness is pervasive," said the middle-aged man whose wife recently died. "I can be in a crowd or by myself, but it's always there. The loneliness seems to bleed through everything else. For me, loneliness comes in only one size — HUGE."

The stress of grief also takes a physical toll. The immune system is compromised. Sleep and appetite habits are disrupted. Our normal routines of attentiveness to physical care are interrupted. We may feel indecisive, disorganized and vulnerable. Preexisting chronic conditions are exacerbated. While these responses may be hard to understand or accept, they comprise a normal part of the grieving process.

Grief is Personal

It's helpful to remember that, just as we have individual fingerprints, we also have individual ways of dealing with loss. Depending upon our personality, we may grieve privately or openly. Grief is also affected by the timing or degree of preparation for the death, and by our previous life experiences. However difficult the process, it's reassuring to realize that grief is actually a therapeutic way to mend a broken heart. It's also important to realize that if we ignore or postpone grief, it may emerge later as a medical condition or a symptom of a mental health problem.

A Guideline Through Grief

I find it's helpful to understand the process of grief by grouping it into three phases. The first phase, which I call Early Grief — THE SHOCK, is marked by initial shock, numbness, and denial. Acknowledging the reality of death leads to the beginning of the second phase, which I call Middle Grief — THE REALIZATION. This is the time when those left behind begin to recognize and experience the impact of their loss. In the final phase, Late Grief — THE RESOLUTION, the bereaved have begun to accept the reality of loss. This is the period when we finally begin to resolve our loss and to give ourselves the necessary permission to begin to move forward and reaffirm our connections with life.

Early Grief — The Shock

"It can't be true! I can't believe it and I just don't know what to do!" the mother exclaimed when she learned of her teenage daughter's fatal accident.

Early Grief, the SHOCK PHASE, begins when we first learn of the loss. Depending on the nature of the death, this period can last a short time or persist for weeks, even months. In Early Grief we experience initial denial, disbelief, shock, numbness, and emotional confusion. We recognize cognitively, in our minds, that the person has died, but we aren't yet ready to believe it in our hearts. Actually we don't want to believe it! In this phase we are not only confronted with the fact that the death has occurred, we also must address concerns related to final arrangements, a funeral or memorial service.

Funerals and Memorial Services — Caring for the Living and Paying Tribute to the Dead

There are many decisions to be made in the Early Grief period. The most time-sensitive issue is the funeral. Will we have a traditional funeral, a memorial service, or a personal, private commemorative ceremony? Will there be earth burial or cremation? If we choose cremation, what will we do with the ashes? Each decision is difficult to make. Each is a "forever decision."

Religious, cultural and personal rituals and beliefs contribute to the final decisions we make. At these times such rituals serve an important purpose. They provide the structure and guidelines which give us an expectation of how to behave and how to proceed. Whether the final ritual is formal and ceremonial, or personal and informal, a ritual provides us with comfort and a sense of purpose.

Jayne found herself in a position she'd never anticipated. "My husband died suddenly. My two teenagers and I struggled to make sense of it all. What were we to do? I had no preparation. I realized we were creating new family rituals for losses to come in the future. After meeting with a funeral director and discussing all the issues, the kids and I literally drove around to several cemeteries to look at cemetery lots. We took our time making the final arrangements and now as I look back, I am glad the kids and I talked everything over and made the decisions we did. Those early-on decisions have a long-lasting and healthy impact on our family."

It's been my professional experience that we share a popular expectation that a funeral or memorial service will finalize our grief and help to provide "closure." Generally, despite the strength of the word "closure," that is not the case. This state of mind is difficult to achieve.

I believe a funeral or memorial service does serve significant purposes.

At one level, a formal observance provides an opportunity to honor the life of our loved one who has died. At a second level, the service offers a setting, whether spiritual or secular, where we can receive and accept the support, friendship and love of family, friends, neighbors and co-workers. It's a time to come together, sharing meaningful memories and discussing what has occurred in our lives. In short, the funeral provides reality, and reality heals!

At her father's funeral, Sandy heard, for the first time, endearing stories about him. "It was so wonderful. At Dad's funeral, his hunting buddies stood up and told great stories I'd never heard before. Some were funny, others heroic. I got to see and know my Dad in a new, beautiful way."

Middle Grief — The Realization

The casserole dishes have been returned and the dining room table is still piled high with papers. "Even though I sit by my telephone, no one calls," the grieving widow sighs. "Where did everyone go? Now I know it's real, and I really feel lost and alone."

In Middle Grief — The REALIZATION PHASE, the shock and denial have diminished. The loss is now real. Yes, we yearn for the telephone to ring, to share our story with someone, or maybe to even taste another tuna noodle casserole.

We become confused. Some days we feel OK and other days we seem to feel worse. Those around us expect us to be doing better by now. We expect it of ourselves. A caring daughter called me expressing concern about her mother, a widow of nine months. "I don't get it! At the funeral she did so well. She took care of everything. Now she can hardly take care of herself. What is happening to my mother?"

In Middle Grief, when we realize the full impact of the loss, our daily life can become overwhelming. We may feel helpless and disorganized. It's frustrating and also tempting to deny or postpone the overwhelming pain. However, this is the time when we need to give ourselves the permission to accept the reality of loss.

A teenager whose father had died, wistfully asked me: "Hey, why can't

I just jump over this part; you know, go from my Dad's funeral to feeling better?"

"Why?" I tried to explain. "Unfortunately, that would be like putting a bandage over an open wound without first treating the infection. You can't see the wound, but it's not healed yet."

Late Grief — The Resolution

"At times, grief feels like a dull ache, but I'm stronger now," said the young man whose partner had died of AIDS. "Finally, I feel more positive about life."

Gradually, without fan fare, we move into Late Grief, the RESOLUTION PHASE. We're feeling better, a little happier, enjoying renewed energy and moments of peace and clarity. We find we have fewer tears and more smiles. We feel stronger physically. We're not as lonely and out of step as we were before, and once again we're becoming involved in life. We may even feel we're gaining control over our lives again.

Small glimmers of hope and relief, enjoying a laugh shared with friends, may sometimes be followed by a guilt-trip. "Should I be feeling better?" a widower asked me. "Is this OK?"

I reassured him: "Relax, it's normal to be asking these questions."

"They say laughter is good medicine," said a man whose child had died two years ago. "I caught myself laughing the other day. Suddenly I realized how long it'd been since I really laughed without feeling guilty. I think I was afraid to turn that corner, to let myself enjoy anything. I guess somehow I thought if I gave in to feeling better, I'd forget my child. Now I realize the end of a life does not mean the end of a relationship."

In Late Grief, we still miss our loved one. However, there is a subtle difference. As we begin to resolve our loss in a healthier way, we also begin to accept the realization that grief is yet another cornerstone in our continuing growth.

"Two years after our teenage son died, my wife and I planned a trip to the Grand Canyon," the father explained. "It was something our boy always wanted to do, and we felt very good about the trip — as though we were taking him with us in our hearts. That feeling let us know we were 'getting better.'"

What Helps Resolve our Grief?

There are three things, in particular, that can help as we deal with grief. They include: granting ourselves permission to grieve, accepting help from others, and exploring information about the grieving process.

PERMISSION — "If we can feel it, we can heal it."

"It's OK!" There is no doubt about it. This simple expression speaks volumes. It is also true that grief is messy and painful. It's natural to want to rush through or postpone it. However, we need the permission to really feel the emotional pain and to allow ourselves the time required to heal that pain.

SUPPORT — "Joy shared is joy increased, and grief shared is grief diminished."

Grief is a lonely journey. But, we can lighten the loneliness of that journey by connecting with others. It's OK to reach out for and accept the support and understanding of family, friends, and members of the community. Think about it. When something good happens we immediately call a friend to share the good news, and the experience becomes even richer in the retelling. Conversely, when something difficult occurs, sharing the sorrow diminishes the sadness. Accepting support from others does not remove the sorrow, but it does soften our feelings of isolation and soothes the sharper edges of grief.

INFORMATION — "Now that I have a guide through grief, I realize I am not going crazy. I'm still normal."

Information gives us understanding. The more we understand how grief affects us, the more in charge we feel. Information is an ally, providing a sense of direction through this life experience. It can come from loved ones, friends, caring professionals, even a sympathetic neighbor. Other information resources include: the Internet, national and local self help services, churches, community organizations and groups, literature, books, and media resources (See Chapter Six: Who Can I Call? Resources for Loss and Bereavement, Trauma, and Chronic Illness).

SUSAN'S STORY

"My son's death taught me how to live"

"There I was in the hospital, cradling Jamie in my arms, as he took his last breath. I remember realizing that some day all of us have to die. I can think of no better place to leave this world than in the arms of someone who loves you"

- Susan, Jamie's mother

Susan's Story, which follows, describes the three phases of grief, beginning with her initial response to her son's tragic accident. She retraces her journey through the hopeless wilderness and impact of her grief. As she begins to resolve her loss, she also emerges with a new appreciation for the smallest gifts of life. Susan paints a picture with the honesty, clarity and insight that she was not privileged to have years earlier, at the time of Jamie's death.

She speaks candidly as she looks back on her life following Jamie's death: "Jamie was seven when he died. If I'd understood more about the effects of grief then, I would have felt less confused and lost. What I was going through was normal grief, but I didn't know that. Almost 30 years later, I have a different vision. Today, I realize that my grief has left me with understanding and hope. Maybe my words can help another bereaved parent feel less alone."

If you were to meet Susan today, you'd see an attractive, confident, outgoing woman with an easy smile and a sparkle in her green eyes. This is so different from the despondent young mother who, at one time, struggled to make it through just one more day.

The following, in her own, personal words, is Susan's story.

To tell my story, I have to go back into the darkness and grief I struggled with for so long. I don't know about other parents, but when Jamie died, my world came to a crashing halt. My grief took me all over the place. I barely functioned at the time. I wasn't sure I could go on living. I felt so despondent. I would never have believed that I might come out of it with a greater appreciation of what's really important. I still miss Jamie very much, but now it's in a different way.

Early Grief — "This can't be happening!"

THE ACCIDENT — You get a phone call. There has been an accident. Your child dies. Your life, as you knew it, is forever changed.

It was late Friday afternoon, the beginning of Labor Day weekend. I was preparing dinner — I remember I was cooking chicken. My mother and Step-Father had just arrived from Florida for a family wedding. A neighbor had invited my two older boys, Jamie, seven, and Denny, nine, to go swimming. Our baby, Michael, who was almost two, was home with us.

It was close to 4:20 when the telephone rang. It chills me to remember the voice. It was a call from the county sheriff's department telling me there had "been an accident." I was told to go to the emergency area of the hospital. Even though I urgently pushed him for details, the caller left no opportunity for questions. If I received a call like that today, I'd demand answers — because when they don't tell you any details, it's only normal to fear the worst.

We raced to the hospital, getting there before Jamie's ambulance arrived. I guess they worked on him at the lake a long time before they brought him to the hospital. When the ambulance pulled in, I rushed out to meet it. I knew it was bad when I saw him. No one knew just what happened at the lake or how he drowned, but he didn't regain consciousness.

Looking at him, lying there, I just wanted to do something myself! Even though everything was being done, and there was nothing I could do, I still wanted to help. I was his mother and that's what mothers do! It's terrible to feel so helpless, so powerless!

Hospital Vigil

What happens to a parent at a time like this?

Jamie was transferred to a specialized children's hospital. I moved into the Ronald McDonald House, a residential facility adjoining the hospital, which is available for families of critically ill children. Most of my time was spent in Jamie's room.

He was on life support systems from Friday until his death four days later. I couldn't leave Jamie's side. I had a feeling from the beginning he wasn't going to make it.

It's odd the things I remember about the four-day vigil at the hospital. I was cold all the time, and wore a sweater constantly! I shiver now even thinking about it. And, I remember how strange it was that, except for all the medical equipment surrounding him, Jamie looked "OK." His color was normal, his hair was combed, and I really couldn't see any visible marks on him.

Standing there, looking down at him in the bed — Jamie looked so small. It was hard being next to him and not having him close to me, or even holding his hand. His body was surrounded by machines, tubes and IV's, so the best I could do was kiss his forehead.

The Final Good Bye

On the second day, the doctor said Jamie was "getting worse." He spoke gently about removing the life support and of his own belief in life after death. He said he felt that in Jamie's case, a spiritual kind of death had already occurred. In a compassionate way, he suggested "it was time to let go." The doctor explained there would be a gradual cutting back of medication and life support over two days.

I'd had the feeling Jamie wasn't "there" anymore. I didn't know you could get worse, but there were signs from the brain scans, and from the dilation of his pupils. My instinct was to just rip all those tubes and things out of him and let him be. It may sound strange, but when you see your child like that, the decision isn't hard to make. The final decision felt like — please don't do this to him anymore!

From the beginning, I had desperately wanted to hold Jamie in my arms. When the time came to remove his life support, I asked the doctor if I could hold him as he died. The doctor agreed. I quietly waited in the hall while life support systems were removed, and then was ushered back into the room. A very kind nurse had brought in an armchair. I sat down and they carefully placed Jamie in my arms.

In two or three minutes he stopped breathing. I could feel the life draining out of him. He was warm, then suddenly felt cold against me. Spiritually I'll never really know if he died in my arms, but he did stop breathing as I held him. I needed to hold him. I remember thinking:

"Seven years ago I brought Jamie into life. Now I need to be with him as he leaves life." I'm so glad I did this. I guess someday we all have to die, and there is no better place to leave this world than in the arms of someone who loves you.

The Funeral

The days following Jamie's death were a blur. We went to the funeral home to make final arrangements. Jamie's older brother, Denny, helped pick out a few personal things to take to the funeral home: clothing to wear in his casket, a soft blanket, and his favorite stuffed animal.

Even though the baby, Michael, was only a year-and-a-half, and unaware of what had happened to Jamie, Michael seemed to shower me with warmth, hugging me, clinging to me in a loving way. That is something I will always remember.

Yet, none of it felt real. There was an outpouring of phone calls, sympathy, and support. Relatives, friends, and neighbors gathered at the funeral home. I stood near Jamie's casket, responding to all the people who came to share their sadness with us. I realized how uncomfortable others were, and it was hard for them to know what to say.

I think we should try to be honest with people in grief, because there are no perfect words. What ever we do to help someone who's grieving, it should be sincere and what we are really feeling. Some of the words or phrases that seem to really help are: "I'm sorry." "I care." "I feel so badly." "I'm at a loss for words." and "I just want to give you a hug."

What I remember being most helpful were the people who — instead of giving advice — offered a touch or hug, or a few words of support. For example, a cousin motioned to me, kind of pulling me out of the "receiving line." I could tell he was struggling to say something profound to make me feel better. Finally he just said: "I love you, Sue. I don't know what else to say."

There were a few things about the funeral that stand out. One was the dress I wore. It was blue and I know it looked nice, but I haven't worn it since. It's still hanging in the closet, and it'll probably hang there forever!

After the funeral and the Mass, we went to Jamie's gravesite. I desperately wanted to be there as they lowered him into the grave. I remember watching the two men as they lowered the casket. Thinking back, I probably made them nervous. They were being careful, slowly releasing the straps that cradled his casket. As they lowered him into the ground I held my breath thinking: "Please don't hurt him."

When the casket was placed in the ground, I put a white rose on top. I realized that others were watching me for a cue to leave, so I slowly turned to walk away. The rest followed. I remember thinking:

"This just isn't right! Parents are supposed to die before their children."

Middle Grief — "Living on empty"

*"Should you shield the canyons from the windstorms
you would never see the beauty of their carvings"*

- Elisabeth Kubler-Ross, MD

Thoughts of Jamie never left me. For months after the funeral, I looked for him everywhere. I'd wander around the house, waiting to hear him calling me. I'd look anxiously for the school bus to pull up at 3:15, only to realize that he would never be coming home on that bus again!

I didn't know much about grief. I was confused. It felt like such a slippery slope. I started at one place, and then I would slide down into a dark valley. It seemed I got worse before I got better. Years later I learned this was normal. It happens as the initial numbness and shock wear off. Then there's no denying the reality of death. It was all so hard to control. I thought I was going crazy!

It was difficult to be around familiar family and friends, much less meet new people and face that question probably every bereaved parent dreads: "How many children do you have?" If I said I had three sons, I'd have to explain about Jamie, and that was never easy. But if I responded that I had two sons, it seemed as though I was leaving Jamie behind, and that felt terrible.

Physically I was a wreck. I was tired all the time. Sometimes I almost felt like I was walking in glue. At one level, I realized that I had the responsibility of maintaining a home and family, but some days it was hard to simply get up from the table and just pour a cup of coffee. I found it hard to eat or even swallow because of a lump in my throat. I lost weight. Looking at my drivers' license photo from that time, I looked like an old, thin, frail woman and I was just 32.

Nothing mattered: having a messy house, answering the telephone, a flat tire, caring about how I looked or what was going on in the world. I wasn't suicidal, but I didn't want to go on living. At night, I'd lie in bed and think about going to sleep and not waking. That would be OK with me. If I died and didn't wake up, at least the pain would be gone.

I was overprotective, worrying obsessively about my two surviving sons and their safety. I'd already lost one son. I couldn't bear losing another. I'd catch myself questioning: "Did Jamie really die?" And the next moment, the whole thing would come crashing back with harsh reality. Everything was a chore. I just couldn't think straight. Emotionally, I was living on empty!

Reflections on Grief

Grief Is Selfish — Without realizing it, I'd become totally self-involved in my grief. I knew other parents had also lost children, but I was so depressed I simply couldn't believe that anyone else could feel worse than I did. How could anyone hurt this badly and still be alive!

Grief became a familiar pain. I worried that if I started to feel better, I'd betray Jamie. I was stuck in my grief because it was so hard to accept that I couldn't go back to the way things had been before. As horrible as my grief was, it had become my safe place. Grief kept me close to Jamie.

"Come on now, isn't it time you pulled yourself together?" Everyone thought I should be "getting over it." Somehow I'd thought after the "first anniversary" passed, I'd either be over it or be dead. Well, a year later I hadn't somehow miraculously died, and I wasn't over it. Now there was no escaping the fact that Jamie was gone forever, and I had to deal with it. If I wanted to have a life, I'd have to make a choice to move forward, to make changes.

Late Grief — "Moving forward"

Today, if someone asked me to name one thing they might do to feel better, I'd tell them this. You're going to have to change something about your life, however small that change may be. You can never go back to the way things were before your child died. I learned this the hard way.

A Path Out of Grief

About a year and a half after Jamie's death, I became concerned about my mother who was living in Florida. I began to realize how hard Jamie's death was on her. I think grandparents have a grief of their own. They hurt in ways others can't understand. There is a double-grief; dealing with the loss of their grandchild, and feeling powerless and sad for their own adult son or daughter.

My mother was also struggling with her loss. She needed me. I decided to visit her, even though I had very little energy of my own and I was nervous about flying to Florida.

Little did I realize that our time together would become the catalyst that helped me out of my own depression. With my Step-Father's encouragement, we made a big effort to get out and do some things. We made plans and we created a little bit of structure together. We did a few 'normal things,' like going out for dinner or doing a little shopping together. By reaching out to help her, I felt better. It was then I realized the value of helping others.

A New Direction

After I returned from Florida, I slowly began to pull myself together. I tried to keep moving forward. I became involved in a Bereavement Ministry at my Parish. Following an intensive bereavement training program, I became certified to help others deal with their personal losses. As I got more involved, I made an exciting discovery. I really had something useful to offer!

Then another opportunity occurred when I accepted a job in a local funeral home working with a bereavement-counseling program. I realized I had the insight, empathy and experience needed to help others. Assisting those who were also dealing with grief became a "spiritual compass" in my life. One day when I was talking with another mother who was very depressed and overwhelmed over the death of her son, I could honestly tell her: "I understand." She hugged me and said, "Yes, I believe you do!"

I finally began to heal. I'd found a new sense of purpose and commitment to others. My energy came back, and now I even felt hopeful.

Finding Significance in Jamie's Death

Here I am, many years later, and I still miss Jamie. But now it's different. If I see a young man in his early 30's who looks like Jamie might look today, or I see a little seven-year old boy with blond hair, freckles and a huge smile, I think of Jamie. Now the hurt is manageable.

I don't think we get over grief. We do get through it. My love for Jamie hasn't diminished; it has grown. Out of his death I discovered a new appreciation for my life and the lives of those I love and treasure.

I've learned to recognize that every year I live — is a special year!

I think poet Robert Browning said it best:

I walked a mile with Pleasure,

She chatted all the way,

But left me none the wiser

For all she had to say.

I walked a mile with Sorrow,

And ne'er a word said she

But, oh, the things I learned from her

When Sorrow walked with me!

CHAPTER THREE

Early Grief

THE SHOCK

"I JUST CAN'T BELIEVE IT.
HAS THIS REALLY HAPPENED?"

"Every transition begins with an ending"

- William Bridges

The Emotions of Initial Grief

Early Grief encompasses the initial response to the death of a loved one. In this period we are confronted with the immediate loss. This phase can last days or weeks, and when the loss is sudden, it may last much longer. We may experience feelings of shock and disbelief, numbness, detachment, denial and in some cases, relief. Other responses normal to Early Grief are: sleep and appetite disturbances, mood swings, guilt, crying, anger, anxiety, and social isolation.

We often find ourselves asking a seemingly endless list of questions. There are so many issues to consider. *What do I do now? Should we have a traditional funeral or a memorial service? My children and I prefer earth burial, but my husband wanted us to cremate him and scatter his ashes. Who has to be notified? How do I tell people that my husband died? Should I say we lost him, or he passed on? It's so hard to say the words "he died."*

First, we must deal with the business of making the final funeral arrangements and attempting to maintain the every day routine. It is not unusual to feel we are functioning on auto-pilot. After the funeral there are insurance and legal forms to be submitted, thank you notes to be written and empty casserole dishes returned to family, friends, and neighbors. Those who are around us may think we are "doing well," because we appear to be taking care of business.

In this period of initial grief we are often only numbly aware of the reality that the death has occurred. Ralph, a recent widower summed it up: "There are miles between my head and my heart. Right now I know I have to stay in my head and make decisions about the funeral. I just can't afford to travel into my heart yet."

When death is the inevitable result of normal aging or a long illness, there may be time to talk about, or even make initial plans. These plans might include a discussion about a traditional funeral, a memorial service or no specific service at all. While talking about "the end" may seem difficult, this discussion can be most helpful to those who will be faced with the responsibility of making final arrangements after the death of the loved one.

When death occurs suddenly or traumatically, we are unprepared for the next step. We may find ourselves in a state of shock, disbelief and confusion as we attempt to make the final arrangements for our loved one.

This is the time when it's helpful to give ourselves permission to reach out to others and accept help. There are many different resources available: close friends and relatives, clergy, funeral directors, doctors, mental health professionals, neighbors, colleagues and community organizations. And, whether it is a private, informal memorial service, a traditional religious service, or an extended public funeral, the final "ceremony" should meet the personal needs of each family.

People approach me and ask what they might do to help their sister, for example, when a child dies? There are many tangible ways we can express ourselves. Providing a warm hug or simple expressions of kindness mean a great deal. There are no "magic words" in expressing our condolences. The two simple words that say the most remain: "I care."

It should be noted that the funeral or memorial is a one-time event. There are no rehearsals or instant replays. This is our final opportunity to place our own personal imprint on this ceremony. This is the time to follow our hearts.

Providing comfort and support to the grieving family extends after the funeral. Bereaved families appreciate acts of kindness long after the initial period of grief. Bud and Esther's son, Michael, an active duty soldier, died in combat. Much time and effort were involved in shipping Michael's body back to the States and in planning his military funeral.

Several weeks after Michael's funeral Bud and Esther found themselves exhausted and confronting an emptiness they had not anticipated. Then something unexpected happened. Bud explained: "It was some time after Mike's funeral. One afternoon one of Mike's good friends from the service called to say he and several buddies were in town. He wondered if the boys could come by to visit with us. We had food and shared tears and laughter. A lot of stories were told. Finally, it was time for them to go. While it was hard to see them leave, Esther and I felt such comfort in their visit. The best part was they hadn't forgotten our son. The boys may never understand how much their visit helped us through our grief."

In consideration of death on the battlefield, I am reminded of the words of William Manchester, recounting his World War II experiences in his book, <u>Goodbye, Darkness</u>. Manchester commented: "Violent death, including death on the battlefield, is unsparing on next of kin. The man killed in action cannot observe the five stages, so those who loved him must do it for him, or at least try to. Those who succeed are fortunate, and few. I wrote many letters to the parents of Marines who had died in my section. One came back from the mother of an Iowa horticulturist. She was furious with me because I was alive and her son was not. I envied her; she was passing through a strengthening catharsis."

The six stories in this chapter describe how, in Early Grief, numbness and denial can interrupt the lives of those left behind. The voices in these stories resonate shock and disbelief, regret, guilt and even a sense of calm and relief.

Carla and Robert vividly remember each detail of the emergency telephone call informing them of their college-age son's accident. The attending emergency physician went "beyond the call of duty" to help the parents confront their loss.

Bobby's father pays a tender, loving tribute to his eight-year-old son. The young Cub Scout has had a fatal accident, and his father brings Bobby an unexpected gift.

When Grandpa Walter dies, little Beth just has to find a way to tell Grandpa a most important thing. Beth speaks the words of universal grief when she says: "Grandpa, I just want to see you one more time, for one more day."

As Henry's wife, Frances, struggles with Alzheimer's Disease, Henry grapples with ways to cope with the physical and emotional changes that affect his Sweetheart of so many years. He quietly admits that "Living with Frances was like living with a silent ghost."

While Violet doesn't find the answers she so desperately seeks from her husband Edward's suicide note, she does find a new way to reconcile her grief.

At age 17, Eric's father has died suddenly and now Eric feels he's also lost his mother whose grief is all-encompassing. Everything in his life is now upside down and he worries about the responsibility of becoming the "man of the house."

CARLA AND ROBERT
"WE'LL NEVER FORGET THE NIGHTIME EMERGENCY PHONE CALL"

"An accident?" Those two words of an emergency phone call
forever resonate with loved ones

A year after their son died in a car accident, Robert and Carla are still remembering the events. It began with the shrill ring of the telephone in the middle of the night.

"It's all been so unbelievable," Carla said. "In the past year, I've told 'the story' over and over. Maybe it's my way of wrapping my arms around it, coming to grips with it all."

"It was such a sudden shock," Robert continued. "I remember it like it was yesterday. When the phone rang I glanced at the digital clock. It was 1:00 AM. I flipped on the nightstand light and anxiously picked up the receiver. I'm not even sure I said hello."

"As I look back," Robert reflected, "I realize the doctor calling me had used a step-by-step process in the way he delivered his bad news. He gradually eased me down into the worst part, because when I answered the phone, a voice with modulated authority asked: 'Is this the Smith residence? Do you have a son at Central College?'

"Who's calling," I asked. "Yes, this is Robert Smith, and yes, my son, Jacob is a Junior at Central College. What's going on?"

The man on the phone continued: "This is Dr. Miller of Central Hospital Emergency Department. I'm sorry to tell you that there's been an accident. Could you come immediately?"

I couldn't believe what I was hearing. "ACCIDENT? What do you mean? Jacob? In an accident? Oh my God, is he all right?"

"It's very serious," Dr. Miller said. He went on: "Please, bring someone with you. How long will it take to get here?"

"My wife and I will be there in two hours," I told him. " What do you mean by very serious?"

There was a slight pause. Dr. Miller said: "Jacob was in a car accident. I'm afraid his condition is critical. Come immediately. I'll be waiting for you."

"NO! This can't be happening," I yelled into the receiver. "There must be some mistake!"

There was no mistake!

It was a parent's worst nightmare.

Robert and Carla dressed and left the house immediately. The two-hour drive to Central Hospital was an eternity. Carla leaned on her husband's shoulder digging her fingernails into his right arm as he drove.

Dr. Miller was waiting at the hospital emergency entrance. As they ran toward the double doors, he approached them. With one hand on each of the parent's shoulders, he guided them to a small room.

He closed the door and urged them to sit down together at a table. The doctor pulled a box of tissues from a shelf and placed it on the table. Speaking slowly and in measured words, he delivered the news as a series of critical facts: "Jacob was driving on the freeway this evening. He was driving at a high rate of speed. It appears he was alone."

Dr. Miller paused, reaching across the table, carefully sliding the tissue box toward Carla and Robert: "Apparently your son's right front tire had a blow out. He lost control of the car and flew off the road, hitting the cement structure of an overpass. When Jacob's car hit the cement abutment, it caught on fire. A passing car called 911. Jacob suffered extensive burns over most of his body."

Carla interrupted: "Where is he? Please, just take us to him now!"

"I know you want to see him, but I must prepare you," Dr. Miller paused. "To prevent infection, Jacob's been placed in an enclosed room, a sort of sterile tent. You can't get close to him. However, you can see him through the window in the next room, and you can speak to him through a microphone. I honestly don't know if he will hear you, but please try to talk to him, just in case."

Robert interrupted the doctor: "What are you really saying?"

"Jacob's prognosis is grave. The chances that he will make it through this don't look good." the doctor quietly said. " If you're ready, I'll take you to him now."

Dr. Miller led the parents through the hospital corridors and into a small room in the intensive care wing. Through a glass window they could see Jacob lying motionless in a hospital bed, his body wrapped in sterile gauze like a mummy. He was on a ventilator.

"My heart stopped when I looked through the glass," Robert said. "All I could see was Jacob's nose. I wanted to bang against the glass! I was desperate to race in there to get to him, to lift him off that bed and take him home."

Carla spoke softly: "I just wanted to climb in the bed with him and hold him in my arms. I wanted to comfort him, to whisper soothing words. I didn't want him to die alone." She swallowed: "I'm so grateful for my faith. I just knew at that time only God could help him."

Following Dr. Miller's suggestion, Carla and Robert each spoke to Jacob through the microphone. They held onto one another tightly as they took turns speaking to their son. They told Jacob how much they loved him and gave him permission to let go. As they spoke to Jacob through the glass, they watched the monitor above his head, hoping to see some signs of life. There was no movement.

He died within an hour after his parents' arrival that night.

Here they were a year later, remembering and revisiting the shock, disbelief, and sorrow. Their grief had started with that telephone call from the emergency room of the hospital. Twelve months later, every nuance of that entire night remained vivid in their minds

Robert confessed: "To this day, if the phone rings after 11:00 in the evening, I worry that it'll be bad news."

"How much worse it could have been, " Carla continued, "if we hadn't been alerted to Jacob's critical condition!" She paused, "Thank goodness Dr. Miller was the attending physician that night. We didn't realize it at the time, but we were so fortunate that we was there. He had the foresight to prepare us as much as possible. He really helped guide us along, encouraging us to give Jacob 'permission to let go' and most of all, giving us a final chance to tell our son how much we loved him."

BOBBY
"You finally got your suede jacket, son"

The room was silent and still. The scent of fresh flowers permeated the air. The tall man, making an obvious effort to stand erect, walked slowly, grimly up to the casket, moving almost gingerly for a man of his large size. He stood in front of the dark wood casket, staring into the youth's face. Bobby, who just turned eight, looked as though he was sleeping.

The father's mind flooded with painful memories. He shook his head. It had happened so quickly. A senseless accident. Bobby was riding his bicycle, coming home from the playground, and was hit by a car.

The intensity of the father's pain was reflected in his eyes. "Why?" he whispered in anguish.

"It isn't fair, my son, my little Cub Scout. Dear God, kids don't die before their parents!"

The father's hand moved slowly over the boy's cheek, then down his shoulder, mindlessly rubbing the leather fringe on the arm of the boy's new suede jacket. It was Bobby's dream jacket, and he'd written it on his wish list for Christmas and his birthday. For years Bobby had begged for a soft suede jacket with fringe, "You know, Dad, I want the kind like

Buffalo Bill wore in those old cowboy movies!"

His parents thought it was too expensive, too extravagant. None of the other kids wore them. But Bobby didn't care what other kids wore, and he continued to ask for the jacket. He was fiercely independent, and "marched to his own drummer" as his father would say. Other gifts were substituted, Bobby politely mumbled a thank you and continued to fantasize about wearing the soft tan jacket, fringe swishing in the wind as he rode his bicycle through the neighborhood.

Now Bobby was cradled in his casket, wearing his new suede jacket with fringe on it.

The father heaved a deep sigh. He tried to straighten up and regain his composure.

"Well, you got your jacket, son," he mumbled, and strained to hold back his tears. He leaned down toward Bobby, gently touching his son's cheek." Bobby, I'm just sorry that we didn't get this for you sooner."

BETH

"GRANDPA, I JUST WANT TO SEE YOU ONE MORE TIME, FOR ONE MORE DAY"

"Oh no, Grandpa Walter is dead?
Where is dead anyway?"

- *Beth, age nine*

Should we tell children about death? Yes.

Parents may feel their children are too young, needing protection from crisis and loss. Most children, however, are resilient and able to deal with adversity when guided by adults. Even if they don't fully understand, children often have an intuitive sense when something is wrong in the family. In their youthful way, they want to know the truth about what is happening. Excluding them isolates them from the family. It fosters insecurity, and forces them to find answers from their own limited life experience. When we include children in family events, such as weddings and funerals, they feel more secure and emotionally stronger. As they learn to deal with loss and death, children learn to deal with life.

Claudia and her husband Brian had three young daughters, ages eleven to six. When Claudia's father died, she and Brian discussed what they should do and how they should tell their children. They made the decision to be completely honest. They sat down with the girls and quietly told them: "Grandpa Walter has died. Tomorrow there will be a funeral to say goodbye to Grandpa. Some people will tell stories about him, even funny ones. Other people will be very sad and cry because everyone is going miss him. Let's put on our dress up clothes, and we're all going together to say goodbye to Grandpa."

Of the three girls in the family, nine-year-old Beth was the exuberant one. She dove into life full sail. She was vividly alive with her feelings and freely expressed both joy and sorrow. Beth was passionately close to her Grandpa Walter. When he died, she simply was not ready to let him go.

Claudia talked about the night before her father's funeral. "Brian and I were closing up our home for the night. It was very late. We noticed a light still on in Beth's bedroom. I peeked in and saw her lying in bed with her lap-pad, positioned against her folded knees. She was frantically writing. Tears were streaming down her cheeks. Beth looked up at me, shaking her head, and said she just couldn't talk. She was writing a letter to Grandpa! I blew her a kiss and closed her bedroom door. I made a mental note to make a photocopy of Beth's letter in the morning before the funeral, as I thought she might like a copy for her memory box.

The next morning, as we were preparing to leave for the funeral, Beth asked me for a large envelope for her letter. She said she had important things to put in the envelope: things like a picture of herself and a picture of the family, some rubber bands and masking tape, because Grandpa was always fixing something and he would need them, and a special picture of Grandma, because she was so upset when Grandpa died. I knew she wanted to personally give her letter to her Grandpa, and I suggested she wait until the end of the funeral, so the two of us could go up to his casket privately."

Tears welled in Claudia's eyes as she remembered. "During the funeral service, Beth sat in the front row next to me, fidgeting with her envelope. At the end of the service she watched everyone stand up, file past the casket and leave the room. We were the last two. Frantically, Beth looked up at me, waving the envelope in her hand and nodding her head toward the casket. I realized she was afraid she wouldn't get her chance to say goodbye.

I took her hand and together we walked up to Grandpa's casket. Beth begged me to pick her up, to 'give her a boost.' I did, so she could get closer toward my Dad. She leaned way down into the casket, putting her letter into his hands. Then, cupping his face with one hand on each cheek, Beth held his face in the gentle gesture of love I had seen her use so often with her Grandpa.

Before I realized it, Beth lunged forward from my arms in toward his casket. Tears running down her face, she encircled her Grandpa's head within her small arms. Messing up his hair and the make-up carefully applied by the funeral director, Beth lifted Grandpa Walter's head right off the pillow. She bestowed her last, most loving, goodbye kiss on his lips."

At age nine, Beth exemplifies the purity of love and grief. Beth's parents, with great insight, gave their daughter permission to express her grief in her own way. As she spontaneously bent down into the casket, tenderly holding Grandpa Walter's face in her hands for that one last kiss, Beth was sharing her love in her own heartfelt way.

Beth's words in the following letter to her Grandpa express the words of universal grief: "I just wish I could see you just one more time, just for one day."

'Hi' Grandpa

So, what's up? In Heven.
I hope every body up there
Loves you as much a I do
who coudn't not Love you
your so nice and sweet and
so, so Handsom I love you
a lot and I miss you so, so,
so, much. and I love you
so, so, so, so much. Have
you gulf-ed or bowled yet
& I hope your having fun
Grandma is really upset I
just wish I could see you
Just one more time just
for one day I dont think
you ever got to hear me
play piano I think I'm getting
pretty good I just miss you
So much right know Well
I have to go know, oh and
if you can, please give me a
sign that you got up to Heven
O K.
            Love your Grandchild
                Beth

HENRY

"Living with Frances was like living with a silent ghost"

When a loved one dies unexpectedly, families are consumed with shock and disbelief. Conversely, when death occurs after long-term illness, loved ones may be sadly resigned to the loss, and in some cases, reluctantly relieved that the suffering has ended.

"My wife died of Alzheimer's Disease," Henry explained. "I took care of her for seven years. Earlier in her illness Frances was childlike and mischievous. As her disease progressed, she became quietly distant, and for a long time she just wasn't there. It was like living with a silent ghost! Grief became part of my daily life. Don't get me wrong, I love her and miss her terribly, but I had to say goodbye to Frances years ago."

As we approach midlife, we become more aware of our friends or a family member struggling with Alzheimer's disease, often called "The Long Goodbye." The emotional grief often occurs long before the final loss. While a cure has yet to be found, there are treatments for symptom management and numerous support services for patients and caregivers.

Alzheimer's is a "family disease." When one person in the family is diagnosed with Alzheimer's disease, everyone in the family is affected. The struggle with the uncertainties of the disease is constant, as the disease claims the mind, body and spirit of their loved one.

One afternoon a young man, Ted, called my office, expressing urgency in his situation. "I don't know how we arrange this, Doctor," he started, "but our family needs a grief counselor. My Mom just died. Mom and Dad were married 65 years. My sister and I feel terrible, but my Dad acts like nothing happened. Sis and I are wondering what's going on here? We thought they had a good marriage. Mom was sick for seven years, and now she's dead and he shows no emotion. We're pretty concerned about him. Could you please meet us at the funeral home and talk with him?"

The day before the scheduled funeral service, I went to the funeral home to meet with the family. Ted's father, Henry, was sitting stoically in a wing chair, next to his wife's rosewood casket. His small, thin frame appeared lost in the chair. He wore a dark gray suit that must have fit him well several years ago, but now hung limply over him. His white dress-shirt fit loosely around his neck. I had the feeling he didn't really mind how he looked. He appeared to be somewhere else.

Typically, in funeral home visitations, the family stands near the casket to greet all those who come to pay respects. This was not the case with Henry. He remained seated in the large chair near Frances' casket, even when someone approached. The top half of the casket was open, framing a serene Frances, a rosary draped in her folded hands. A large floral arrangement of her favorite flowers, Black Eyed Susans and lush white Daisies, rested on the lower closed section of the casket, and an array of hand-colored cards with pictures and notes of goodbye from her four grandchildren surrounded the flowers.

I pulled up a chair next to Henry and introduced myself. I told him that his children were concerned about him and had asked me to come and talk with him. "This must be difficult for you, Henry," I said.

He looked at me. "I know my kids called you. They try, but they just don't understand how it's been for the past several years. Unless you've been though it, you can't understand. I shielded my kids from the rough stuff. Taking care of Frances was my job, not theirs." He took a deep breath and continued:

"Some people call Alzheimer's 'the Long Goodbye.' I agree. It seemed so long. I am tired and sad and relieved. Frances was not my Frances for many years. She was living and breathing, but not there at all! Don't get me wrong, I don't begrudge taking care of her — not for one minute. But at times she was a real handful! Earlier in her illness, she was like a child, always into mischief. I had to watch her all the time so she wouldn't turn on the stove or fall down the stairs. I had to bathe, diaper, dress and protect her. She was my responsibility. The buck stopped with me. I've lived on hyper-alert for years."

Henry paused and took a deep breath. "One afternoon I was in the kitchen making stew for dinner. Frances always took an afternoon nap so I assumed she was resting in bed. The kitchen phone rang. The call was from a concerned neighbor who lived three blocks away. The neighbor had discovered Frances in the back yard of her house, looking at the garden. Frances was wearing her bathrobe and a pair of white ankle socks. She had no identification and didn't know who she was or where she lived. Fortunately, the neighbor's son recognized her, as he delivered the newspaper to my home.

Immediately I drove over to pick her up. I was concerned and embarrassed. That episode was the turning point. Now I realized there were new problems to face. Soon after that incident I installed better locks on the inside and outside of the doors."

Henry looked over at his wife in her casket. "Another day Frances set her robe on fire! I was in the basement doing laundry when I heard her shriek. I ran up the stairs to see her standing there, holding a box of wooden matches, her terry cloth robe aflame. Quickly I doused the fire, led her to the couch and quieted things down. Then, I child-proofed the house; hiding matches, sharp objects, knives, scissors, and tools."

The constant surveillance, however, was hard on Henry. The children offered to help and the Senior Center provided "sitters," so he could go to the barbershop, the bank and grocery without worrying. From time to time Henry reluctantly hired helpers. " It was such an effort. Frances wore adult diapers. Like a little child, she would play with the contents of her diaper and make a mess all over the place. Before the sitter would come I'd change Frances' diaper and put her in fresh clothes. But, she was always a mess when I got home. Even when I had a sitter, I just couldn't relax. It was supposed to be a break for me, to go out and not worry. But I worried all the time. When I was away I worried that somehow she would miss me and be frightened," he lowered his head. " She probably didn't even know I was gone. I'll never know."

"It just wore me down. Who could I talk to about this stuff? Not my kids. I was her husband, her caretaker. I loved Frances! We had 65 years together. In the last years she'd become docile, like a ghost. I couldn't talk with her about anything; not the good old days, or our kids, or even about her dying."

Here at the funeral home, the day before he was to bury his wife, Henry expressed how he felt: "I want the children and grandchildren to share happy memories, to tell the stories of the Frances who loved to sing and dance. This is time to say our last good bye." He looked at me and said softly: "Do you understand now why I appear so calm? It isn't that I don't care. It's that I've been grieving for my Sweetheart for years. I did everything I could, and I'm really OK with things. I have to try to move forward now."

I asked him about his plans for himself, following the funeral. He admitted that he had given the matter considerable thought. He talked about volunteering for an Alzheimer's support group where he could help others who were in the same struggle. Getting involved in something out in the world was important to Henry. He'd been considering church, a widowed group, and maybe playing some golf or fishing.

"Frances would want me to be involved in life again," he said.

Henry looked at me, smiled and said: "It's OK. Frances is at peace now and so am I."

VIOLET

"In my husband's suicide note, I was looking for answers that weren't there"

The aftermath of her husband's suicide left Violet mired in frustration, sadness, guilt, anger and unanswered questions.

Violet invites us into the prison of her guilt and confusion, as she reads and re-reads her husband's suicide note — looking for answers that aren't there. In the process of dissecting Edward's note, she discovers that her grief moves from the obsessive question of "Why did he do it?" to "What can I do to resolve my loss?"

Violet's husband Edward killed himself with his service revolver in the basement of his home.

Violet had been out doing her Monday morning shopping. When she returned, she put the groceries away and began her routine morning tasks, starting with the laundry. The house was quiet. She had called out to Edward, but there was no answer. She assumed he'd stepped next door to see his buddy, Frank.

Violet emptied the laundry hamper into her basket and, with the basket in her arms, navigated her way down the narrow basement stairs. It wasn't until she reached the bottom step that she saw Edward's body in the far corner of the basement. He was slumped in a strange position on the floor, covered in blood. The blood had splattered on the white stucco walls above his head.

Dropping her laundry basket, she shrieked and ran to him. With the edge of her cotton apron, she wiped the blood off his neck and pressed her two fingers against him, feeling for a pulse. She felt nothing. Holding the stair railing, Violet managed to get herself up the stairs to the kitchen phone to call 911.

Police and an ambulance arrived quickly. Violet recognized one of the officers, as he'd attended Edward's retirement party last year. He was kind, urging her to sit down at the kitchen table and talk with him. He told her Edward was dead and that they would be taking him to the local hospital for examination. He said there would be paperwork to complete, but first he wanted to call her son, Todd.

As soon as Todd arrived, the policeman explained the situation, and completed the necessary paperwork with both of them. After the officer left, Todd and Violet went back downstairs. He approached his mother, giving her a strong, reassuring hug and said gently: "Mom, the officer found a note taped behind the bottom basement stair. He gave it to me, suggesting we look at it together, but only when you are ready." He placed the note in her hand.

As she tucked the note in her apron pocket, Violet noticed the blood on her hands. "Good Lord, Todd, look at my hands!" Leaning over the cast iron laundry tub, she watched the blood, trickle down into the tub, turning from bright red to pink, and down into the drain.

She caught her breath: "Oh, dear God, WHAT has just happened here?" she asked herself.

The following days remained a blur. There was a funeral. Violet numbly went through the motions of burying her husband of 42 years. In the weeks that followed, her son, Todd, and the neighbors, especially Frank, Ed's buddy, came over to help her out. There was so much to do, yet Violet felt immobilized. She felt the tasks were endless: filling out insurance and veteran's forms, dealing with Edward's Trust, paying bills, and the overwhelming job of sorting out Edward's clothes and tools. Neighbors brought meals over every day.

Violet struggled to pull herself together, but the question remained: WHY? She read his note over and over. There was nothing there. She tried to put the pieces together. What had she missed? Was Edward so unhappy that he just wanted to die? He'd retired from the police force a year ago. Lately, he had been depressed and more quiet than usual — but nothing that led her to think he would kill himself.

Several weeks after Edward's funeral, Violet called asking if, in my capacity as a grief counselor, I could visit her. She wanted to talk about Edward. Grief was overwhelming her and as hard as she tried, she just couldn't come up with any answers as to why Edward took his life. He'd left her a suicide note, but she could make no sense of it. She was hoping I could help.

Violet greeted me warmly at the door of her tidy bungalow. She was a small woman, wearing slip-on shoes and a cotton, floral print apron over her housedress. Her glasses seemed to cover her face. We exchanged pleasantries.

After a short time she asked if I'd be willing to talk about Edward's suicide. Would I go downstairs where it happened? She said: "I had NO idea he had problems. I feel so guilty. What did I miss? How could I have helped him?" The note he had left made no sense to her. "I've read it so often I think I have it memorized."

Violet led the way down the stairs, turning on the single-bulb basement light by pulling a long piece of string tied to the light switch. She pointed to the bottom stair and asked if we might sit there, as this is where the note was found. We sat side by side on the bottom basement step. Each open-back stair was covered with aged, yellow linoleum. A clean up crew had been hired to clean, patch and paint the blood-spattered basement floor and walls. The basement still smelled of fresh paint.

"It may seem odd to ask you to come down to the basement where I found Ed," Violet spoke sadly, "but I thought maybe it would help us figure out what he was thinking. I often just sit here on this step and cry as I read his note."

I gave her a reassuring smile and said, "Violet, I doubt I can answer your most nagging question of why, but I will be happy to look at Edward's note."

"I had no clue!" she interrupted me. "I did my morning marketing and when I got home, I found him in the basement. I feel so guilty and really don't know what to tell people."

She pushed her glasses up onto her forehead and wiped her tears with a large white cotton man's handkerchief: "I keep going over the note Ed left. It's so cold and impersonal. For the life of me, I can't understand any of this. I thought he loved me. What did I do wrong? I keep thinking I should've done something. I'm just so confused. I can't seem to get this feeling of being responsible out of my head."

Violet pulled the wrinkled, folded note out of her apron pocket and carefully spread it open across her lap. She pushed her glasses down from her forehead and began to read. The note was a simple to-do list of things her husband wanted her to take care of in his absence. Edward signed it: "Love, Ed"

When she finished reading, she looked at me expectantly.

I took a deep breath, and then slowly shared some thoughts. "I wonder if Edward was trying to make sure you'd be OK in his absence? Maybe this note is his way of helping you take care of yourself. Violet, perhaps it's his way of showing his concern and love for you."

She turned the note in different directions on her lap, as if looking for something new on the paper. Softly she said: "I always knew Ed loved me. We were together 42 years, never an argument. He was a policeman most of his life. Then, he was wounded on duty and had to retire early. That was hard on him, even more so lately. The last several months he got pretty quiet," she paused as if trying to recall a memory. " I know he had a lot of pain in his shoulder where he was shot. Maybe he was depressed. I asked him to see a doctor but he wouldn't hear of it. Is there something I should have done? I feel so guilty!"

I touched her arm. "Violet, maybe it's best to remember how much you loved each other. It sounds as though you both did a good job of taking care of each other. Edward may have been in physical pain and possibly depressed. It can happen. You tried to get him to a doctor. Men can be pretty stubborn, you know."

She smiled and agreed: "Stubborn isn't the word for it. I used to tease him and call him one tough cookie. You're right — I DID try to help him. We were good partners."

"I don't think the answers are in his note," I assured her. "We may never know exactly why he took his life, but let's think about something. Edward's act was probably more to relieve his pain, then cause you such grief. I don't think he wanted to hurt you. His note is a list of things you must know to take care of yourself and of the home you and he shared. I think in his way, this was Ed's letter of love."

Violet nodded slowly. She suggested we go upstairs and continue at the kitchen table. She poured a cup of coffee for each of us and we talked some more. "Maybe over time," I suggested, " you'll be able to think less about why he did it, and begin to think about what you can do now to stay healthy. I think Ed would want you to be able to eventually move forward."

Dabbing at her eyes with the now-soaked handkerchief, she replied: "You know what you are saying does make sense to me. Ed was a good policeman and I was his dependable wife. I was even his at-home barber for years! We were hardworking, proud people. I don't think Ed would want me wallowing here. I think he would want me to carry on for both of us."

As I prepared to leave, Violet gave me a big hug and apologized for her tears. I told her something I'd learned about crying: "Tears are little gifts that help us feel better. So cry all you want. It's good for you. It keeps you healthy. Violet, they say that tears add years!"

Violet walked me to her front door, smiled and said:

"Well if you are right about the tears adding years —

I'm going to live a long time."

ERIC

"I'VE LOST MY DAD TO DEATH AND NOW MY MOM TO GRIEF. I FEEL SO ALONE!"

Eric was miserable. His father had died suddenly and his mother was in overwhelming grief. In a very short time his life had completely changed.

"This sucks! I don't want to be the man of the house. I just want my Dad back!"

Eric was 17 when his father died. It was a sudden death, leaving Eric and his mother to work through their grief — each in their own way. It had been several months since the funeral and things were getting worse, not better. Eric, a previously well-behaved teenager, was now skipping school, drinking, hanging out with "the wrong crowd." His mother was concerned about him, and asked me to set up a counseling appointment with him. Feeling Eric would be more amenable to therapy at home instead of a clinical office setting, she asked if I could arrange the meeting there.

I arrived at the front door and was met by a surly, angry young man, whose tall physique blocked the door frame. His arms were tightly folded over his chest. Over his shoulder, loud music blared from the living room. I introduced myself, asking if he remembered we had a meeting today.

He nodded "yes."

A large blue pick up truck was parked in the driveway. I pointed to the truck. "Is that your truck over there, Eric?"

Another affirmative nod.

Still trying to connect with him, I said: "Well, what do you think? Let's go for a ride."

He stared at me: "Why?"

I was relieved. At least he had a voice. "Look, Eric, you're stuck with me for an hour. That's not negotiable. Frankly, I think you might feel more comfortable talking with me in your truck than here on the front porch. What do you say?"

He nodded, grabbed his keys, and we both climbed into the truck. As he backed out of the drive, I volunteered: "Eric, you just drive, go where you'd like to go."

Eric drove. We sat in silence (not an easy task for me!). After some time, he looked over and sneered: "I have nothing to say to you. You might be a nice lady, I don't know and I don't care. The only thing I really know is I want my Dad back. Unless you can make that happen, we have nothing to talk about!"

I didn't respond. I noticed a pile of cassette tapes on the seat (this was prior to iPods and CD's). One tape had a crudely written label, which read: "DAD." I held it up to him inquiringly. "What is your tape?"

He replied; "It's a tape of music I made to be played at my Dad's funeral. It's all that Big Band stuff that my Dad liked." Automatically, he inserted the tape. It began to play.

We both listened in silence for some time.

Breaking Through

I broke the silence by telling him about my work and about other teens. I told him about other kids in grief, some who felt guilty and some who couldn't cry, and some who got very angry. There were many who skipped school, smoked weed, drank, had sex, and basically hated themselves and the world they were living in. He looked over at me, nodding his head. I could tell he was listening.

"How do you know this shit?" Eric asked.

I thought a minute: "It's what I do, Eric. It is my work, and frankly, I feel as strongly and passionately about my work as you do about the loud music you were playing when I knocked on your door." I saw a faint smile creeping across Eric's face. "I really like talking to people who are struggling, because sometimes, just once in a while, something I say seems to make a difference!" I went on: "I'm describing how other kids act and feel because that can help. These are normal things that can happen. Eric, the thing is, you don't have to continue feeling this way."

"Yah, right," he mumbled.

But, from time to time as he drove along, periodically he shot a look over my way and I could tell he was listening. "Look, Eric, there are normal things we go through. I know they don't feel very normal and they can get us in trouble. And, sometimes we just don't even care. When someone dies suddenly, we generally feel numb, in shock, as though we can't believe it. " I paused and he turned down the volume on the music.

I continued: "Then after the funeral, we feel guilty and sad and full of fear. Often we worry that we might have to be the man of the house for Mom, or that now we can't go away to college. We may begin to think we are going crazy. "

"Eric, these are normal things that lots of kids go through!"

Now he was driving slowly. He pulled the truck over into a parking lot and shifted into park. He looked at me. Tears puddled in his eyes. He wiped his nose with his shirtsleeve. "You wouldn't bullshit me, would you? Just to make me feel better?"

I assured him everything I said was true. I asked if he felt some of those things — like being the man of the house and worrying about the future and feeling guilty about his Dad. He agreed to all of it. He said it was all that and more.

The Roadmap

"Eric, there is a way out of this," I said, slightly leaning toward him. "You can get through this. You can't heal something that you don't feel. Talk about it. Talk to your mom, or your uncles, to me, or someone at school. Get back on track with your grades. You'll feel more in control. I can promise you this — if you will do these things, it'll get better. I can give you a guide, a road map. It can work!"

He looked over at me, through his tears and said: "I really didn't even want to meet you! I only wanted my Dad back. I feel like it was all my fault. I was a real jerk to my Dad. I just want to tell him I'm sorry, and now he's gone. In a way Mom's gone, too," he paused looking at me for clarification." She's just not here, not with it all. I feel like I have to be in charge of everything. I hate that my Mom leans on me so much. I miss my Dad every day. And you tell me that is normal?"

I said: "Yes, yes it is, Eric. It is more normal than you think. There are support groups. If you go to one you'll see how much other kids feel this way."

Back in his driveway, he shook my hand and gave me a smile. "You know, Doc, I knew you were coming today and I was prepared to just blow you off. Obviously you wouldn't let me do that. And I think I'm glad. I dunno, maybe you did just give me a roadmap through this grief stuff. I'd like to meet again if we can. Maybe I can do this thing right after all. Anyway, well, at least I'll give it a try."

In the months that followed, I met with Eric two more times. He reported doing better and had signed up to join a support group for grieving teens.

At the closing of the following school year, I received a true gift. It was a short handwritten note from Eric, telling me he was graduating from high school and had a summer job. He said he was doing better, and...

"I just wanted you to know. "

CHAPTER FOUR

Middle Grief

THE REALIZATION

"MY DAUGHTER'S ROADSIDE MEMORIAL
WAS A WAY OF CARING FOR SHANNON
AFTER HER FUNERAL"

"My heart to-day smiles at its past night of tears
like a wet tree glistening in the sun
after the rain is over"

- *Rabindranath Tagore*

Recognizing the Reality of Loss

*"The funeral is over, the flowers have wilted,
casserole dishes are empty, everyone's gone — now what?"*

The memorial or funeral service is over. The physical body of the loved one has been buried or cremated. Out-of-town-family and friends have returned home, the telephone rings less, and there are fewer condolence cards, e-mails, and text messages. Others have returned to their own busy, personal lives.

Our loved one is gone. A new level of grief sets in.

This is the interval I call REALIZATION or Middle Grief. It lingers after the initial loss. It descends upon us some time after the funeral, and, while many don't realize it, this phase of the grieving process can be one of the most difficult. It's the time when we begin to self-doubt. We constantly question ourselves and our behavior. Shouldn't we be doing better? Others seem to expect that of us. We expect it of ourselves. We feel we are making "no progress."

Be assured! It's neither unusual nor abnormal to experience an ebb and flow in the river of grief. We can, and often do, experience intense feelings of loneliness, guilt, anger, and depression. Sometimes the emotional symptoms can lead to physical symptoms, such as dental problems, elevated blood pressure, inability to sleep, or heart palpitations. We are no longer protected by the psychic insulation of initial shock and denial. The fatal bottom line has been reached. Death is now a reality.

Those around us often misunderstand the intensity and duration of our personal grief. It's easy to become confused. They may comment: "Come on, its been several months! You should be getting over this by now!" However, we're not over it. True, we are back to every day life, but we aren't living it.

One day a young man called me, expressing concern about his mother: "Dr. Gilbert," he began, "it's been a year since my Dad died. At first Mom did pretty well, but now she stays home and cries all the time. She's forgetful, disorganized and depressed. We're afraid she's losing it. What should we do?"

There is no timetable for grief after loss. It takes what it takes! During this phase of Middle Grief we may need even more support and understanding than at any other time in the grief journey.

John, a recent widower, explains: "At first I couldn't believe it, but now I know it's real. Initially I was so busy! I had so much to do and I did it. People saw me as taking charge; I guess you can call me a Type-A. Now I can barely move. Yet I feel I have to continue with this phony, brave front. People ask me how I am doing and I say, 'Fine, fine, just fine.' They can't see that, behind my smiling face, I feel really terrible all the time. But, I'm afraid if I confess my overwhelming sadness and loneliness, people would start avoiding me."

Weeks after her husband's death, one widow admitted she was still setting the dinner table for two. Finally, she was able to accept the reality that her husband was never coming home again at the end of the day. It was then that she started setting the table for one and making an adjustment to her new life.

During Middle Grief we may feel misunderstood and isolated from our families and friends. Normal symptoms of this phase can include: loneliness, depression, isolation, emotional ambivalence, anger, and a preoccupation with regret and guilt. We are sometimes disorganized, frantic, and — at times — even a little crazy. We struggle to avoid becoming obsessed by the loss. It's important to realize it's not unusual to have these feelings. While we may have initially functioned well, the eventual reality of death can be overwhelming.

Now, with the erosion of initial shock and disbelief, we are vulnerable. At this time, perhaps more than ever, we really just want to be understood. It may be helpful to seek guidance and support from others.

How good it would feel if someone would ask:

"How are you really feeling?" or "What can I do to help?"

The five stories in this section describe the range of emotions those left behind experience. These stories help us more clearly understand the complexity of life and the pressure loved ones often feel to "get better," to "move forward" and to "go on with it," following a loss.

Tyler returned home from active duty in Afghanistan, not realizing he was carrying "extra baggage." His wife, Amy, worried that although Tyler had returned physically, emotionally he was still a Marine on the front line of war, fighting his personal enemy, invisible grief.

Dot and her husband, Tim, were like "two peas in a pod." In her efforts to deal with Tim's sudden death, Dot tries to bury herself in a whirlwind of activity, feeling she must avoid at all costs, being considered "the grieving widow."

Bill was always the "family fixer," until the day his college-aged daughter, Susan, died of a sudden illness. As he ponders his own grief, Bill finds there is little he can do to fix this loss. Finally, he realizes that "even big guys can cry."

In the months following the death of Shannon, her 16-year old daughter, Kay searches for ways to resolve her grief. It is the creation of a Roadside Memorial, a visible icon of her mourning, that helped Kay move forward in her grief.

Chuck is surprised when his medical doctor strongly urges him to seek "grief counseling" when his health begins to suffer. Until then, he hadn't realized that his emotional problems could have been initiated by unresolved loss.

TYLER
"They say it's PTSD. All I know is nothing's right anymore"

*"Without having the haziest idea of what combat would be, we wanted,
in a phrase which sounds quaint today, to fight for our country"*

- William Manchester

Tyler's War

To escape detection, Amy set her cell phone on "vibrate." She worked for a Certified Public Accountant, and because tax season at an accounting firm is a busy time, her boss had issued an office rule. "No cell phones permitted at work."

She totally understood the rationale for her boss' ruling, but she desperately needed to be available in case her husband, Tyler, called. The best plan, she decided, was to set the cell on "vibrate," and then tuck it under her bra. Now it was near her heart where she could feel its reassuring touch. Carefully, she slid the cell out of her bra and peeked just to be sure it was still turned on.

Amy shook her head. This cell phone was starting to run her life! It never left her side. She tucked it under her blouse at work and set it on the console in her car. Each night, she gently placed it on the nightstand

115

next to her bed, and just to be sure, she recharged it daily.

Now if Tyler called from Afghanistan, she could instantly be in touch. Afghanistan! Years ago, in school, she'd never much learned about Afghanistan or "that part of the world." Now it was all she thought about.

Amy and Tyler met in high school. He played football and she was a cheerleader. They were the "Hallmark card" young lovers. They married soon after graduation. Amy thought it was about as close to a picture perfect wedding as you could get. After two months of marriage, they added a new member to the family; a black Lab puppy. Amy found the puppy to be a lot of work and a source of frustration. But Tyler said no problem, he'd take over the care and training of "his pup" whom he'd named Scout. That suited Amy just fine!

Then, Tyler fulfilled his life-long dream and joined the Marine Corps. He always wanted to be a Marine and Amy supported his decision, never expecting he'd be involved in a war in Afghanistan.

What a war. Tyler was in some God-forsaken country, far from home, fighting an enemy he didn't understand. He was a Marine who described himself as a "killing machine." He was the best. He had a job to do, and he would do it. Yes, she was proud of Tyler, but at the same time, she felt great concern when he was away "fighting for his country."

Soon Tyler would be coming home for good. Amy was nervous about the whole thing. Over a year ago, the last time Tyler was home on leave for the holidays, it was not a good experience!

She clearly remembered that visit, and it wasn't a memory she enjoyed recalling. Amy, her parents and brothers, in-laws and friends had planned a huge surprise welcome home party. Little did she realize then what a mistake that would be! Tyler was in no mood or shape for a party, for seeing his family and friends, or for doing anything at all that day. As a matter of fact, he disappeared in the afternoon, hours before the party.

Earlier that day, while Amy was still cleaning up for the party that would take place without the honored guest, she had heard Tyler screaming. She ran to the bedroom to check on him. The only "normal" thing about the scene in front of her was that the dog, Scout, always Tyler's faithful companion, was on the floor next to the bed. However, bedding was all over the floor. Tyler way lying in his shorts, diagonally across the bed. Beads of sweat peppered his forehead. He was moaning, mumbling something about: "Ugly Hill. That village looks like a ghost town. Hear the sound of the jackals?"

None of it made sense to Amy. She sat on the edge of the bed, gently rubbing her hand against his forehead to comfort him. WHAM! Tyler slammed his forearm against Amy's shoulder, and she fell to the floor.

"Tyler, wake up! You're having a nightmare," she screamed at him. "You just hit me!" Frightened and confused, she ran to the bathroom for a cold cloth and a glass of water. She didn't know what to do — she only wanted him to be "himself" again. When she returned to the bedroom, Tyler was gone.

Amy found him in the kitchen, standing in front of the open refrigerator door, drinking orange juice out of the container. She hated it when he did that, but decided it wasn't worth the argument. She quietly walked up behind Tyler: "We need to talk, Tyler. I don't know what's going on with you and I want to help you. Tell me what I can do!"

He was startled into action. As she spoke, he spun around facing her. "You can leave me the hell alone! I don't want to be here. I'll be better when I get back with my guys. It's not your fault, Amy. I just don't fit in here anymore." Tyler glared at her, "Fer Christs' sake, don't start to cry. I feel bad enough. Don't make it worse." He grabbed the pair of jeans and flannel shirt he'd tossed on the floor the night before, and stormed out the kitchen door.

He didn't return until the next morning. He was hung-over, surly, angry and quiet. He looked terrible and Amy was furious and confused. "What the heck is the matter with you, Tyler?" she cried to him. "All of us worked so hard on this party for you. We were so excited to see you. How could you go off and disappear? Don't you love us?"

There was no answer. Tyler silently looked at the floor. He stumbled to find the words: "Amy, I don't deserve a party. I'm no hero. The real heroes are the guys who didn't make it home. What I saw and did over there isn't worth celebrating."

He kissed her on the forehead and headed to bed. Maybe sleep would make things better.

The holiday did not improve. Tyler put in his time at home, avoiding family and friends, and Amy did her best to avoid confronting him. She had the feeling he was more comfortable around Scout than the rest of the family.

Amy's two brothers, one older and one younger than Tyler, tried to calm her, saying it was just too much for him, coming home in the middle of the holiday season. Her older brother, Brad, advised her: "Amy, hang in there. He's been through things none of us can understand. And he's going back to the middle of it. Just give him some space. Once he's home for good, it'll all work out."

The morning Tyler had to leave to return to Afghanistan, Amy was too upset to go to the airport. She just couldn't see him leave again, so she asked Brad to drop him off.

Two weeks after he left, Tyler called Amy's cell phone. She'd been yearning to hear from him, and, as before, she'd been carrying her cell next to her heart since he'd left. Now she put the phone close to her ear and tried to stay calm. He told her how much he loved her and how sorry he was. He didn't mean to hurt anyone, but everything was all messed up. She could tell he was worried.

He said he felt more "normal" back on the front with his boys! He knew the drill there. They had their own discipline, their own rules. He knew just what to do. He been fighting the war long enough to wonder if that wasn't his "new normal?" As much as Tyler disliked the war, he knew how to survive. Back in the States, he told Amy, he "felt like a stranger." He concluded saying, "Baby, when I come home for good, we'll talk about all of this."

Amy listened intently, trying to muffle her tears. She told him she loved him and couldn't wait for him to finally return.

As Amy awaited Tyler's eventual return home, she took the advice of her family, and arranged an appointment with the pastor of her church. She was worried about Tyler and wanted to help him if she could.

Amy was nervous during the first meeting with the pastor. Although she'd been a long-time member of the church, she'd never had a personal meeting with him. But he instantly put her at ease. Pastor Johnson, it turned out, proved very helpful, as he'd also served in the Marine Corps. And, in no time, she was telling him the whole story of Tyler's recent behavior and her concerns about his return to civilian life.

Pastor Johnson asked about their lives together, and about Tyler's training in the Marine Corps. "Was he a 'Hollywood Marine,' (trained in San Diego)? How much time did she and Tyler spend together before he was deployed?"

He spoke of the conflicts Tyler might be feeling between his time in Afghanistan and back in the States. He tried to help her realize how it is in the military. "Amy, I was a Marine in Vietnam. I had a terrible time when I got back. Many men returned physically, but not emotionally. I suspect that's how Tyler feels, too. In any war, coming back is a tough adjustment."

Pastor Johnson talked about how a Marine's training includes ingrained Codes of Conduct. He stressed that strict discipline plays a pervasive role in a Marine's life, and admitted that his own wife had difficulty, even now, with his strict military-lifestyle.

That discussion resonated with Amy, and she laughingly told him a story. "You're right about being so precise and disciplined. Tyler's always on-me about being organized and being on time. His parents had invited us for dinner one evening. We were to be there at 5:00. At 4:45 I was still doing my hair and getting dressed. He barked at me: 'Let's go!' He grabbed the car keys, started the car and laid on the horn until I finally dashed out the door."

The Pastor gave her a knowing smile. Amy continued: "Tyler calls it 'being squared away.' Everything in his workshop is precisely lined up, tools always put away, very neatly. I think it drives him crazy when I toss my boots and shoes all over the laundry room floor!"

By the end of their third meeting, Amy understood many of the challenges Tyler was bringing home. She felt more prepared for his return than she had at that disastrous holiday a year ago.

The day of return finally arrived. This time the "Welcome Home Party" consisted of Amy, her brothers, her parents, Tyler's parents, and of course, Scout, who'd been Amy's constant companion in Tyler's absence. This intimate group of loved ones quietly welcomed home the Hero they had missed for so long.

Over the next weeks and months, Amy and Tyler walked gingerly around (and about) one another. Tyler had a job working in his Dad's tool and die shop. At Amy's urging, he attended a weekly Veteran's Support Group, specializing in Post Traumatic Stress Disorder (PTSD). Sometimes he even consented to going to church on Sundays with her. One Sunday Pastor Johnson proudly introduced him to the entire congregation. Tyler was embarrassed.

"Old habits die hard," Amy thought. She continued to keep her cell tucked under her blouse at work. She needed that contact with him, and she asked Tyler to call her every day at lunchtime. He dutifully called, but there seemed little to say. Amy could feel the distance in his calls. There was also tension at home. They shared the same bed, but there was no intimacy. Tyler seemed to be walled off in a distant land.

One evening, after yet another dinner in silence, Amy directly asked him: "Tyler what's wrong? Don't you care about anything anymore? Do you miss being over there?"

He took his time answering. He explained that he didn't want to hurt her feelings. After all, she was his wife and he loved her. But nothing felt right, everything was out of sync. He was truly miserable.

Amy was at a loss for words, so she gave him a warm hug and decided to leave him alone.

Tyler's isolation and despondency grew. Finally, he said to Amy: "Amy, you've really been trying to help me. I know that. But I feel lost. I don't know if I miss being 'there,' but I know I don't belong 'here.' I just don't fit."

He stood from the chair, extended his hand to her, and led her to the couch. Pulling her close, wrapping his arms around her, he continued telling her how he felt: "Look, this is so tough. I feel like we're going in circles here! We go to our jobs each day. Every day I call you at noon because you ask me to. We pay our bills and put in our time. Amy, we're both trying to make it work, but that's about it. I look at you and you look so sad and empty. I look in the mirror and I see rage, anger and confusion. Look, I even have to go to the gym every day, just to punch out my frustration on the speed bag."

Amy could feel "it" coming — the inevitable rejection. She wiggled out of Tyler's arms and grabbed the soft pillow tucked in the corner of the couch. She held it against her chest and braced herself for what she was certain would follow.

"I love you, Amy. I have since high school. But our marriage is just not working" Tyler stretched his arm across the couch to hold Amy's hand. "I go to work with my Dad five days a week. I go to the VA support group once a week. Hell, I've even gone to church with you! None of it is working. I'm not working! It isn't you. It's me. I can't do this any more, Amy. I don't fit here, or with you, or maybe anyplace."

Twisting her fingers around the soft fringed-edge of the pillow, Amy choked out the five words she'd been dreading to say aloud: "Do you want a divorce?"

Tyler squeezed her hand, looked directly in her eyes, and then said: "Yes, I think we need to end this marriage."

Several months later Amy and her mother were in the car, driving home from the local Court House. Reluctantly, Amy had signed the final divorce papers. She hadn't lost her husband to another woman. She'd lost him to the war and to PTSD! She'd lost Scout, too, but she'd willingly given the dog to Tyler. She knew Tyler would need Scout close by.

As Mom drove, Amy fiddled around with the car radio, and hit the button of Mom's favorite-station. It was the one that played her special 'golden oldies.'

A song came on. Not realizing the impact of the lyrics on Amy at that particular moment, her mother said: "Oh, Honey, that's a great song! It's from the Civil War. It's about welcoming our soldiers back home. Listen!"

> "When Johnny comes marching home again, Hurrah! Hurrah!
> We'll give him a hearty welcome then, Hurrah! Hurrah!
> The men will cheer and the boys will shout
> The ladies they will all turn out
> And we'll all feel gay
> When Johnny comes marching home."
>
> *- Patrick S. Gilmore (1863)*

At the end of the song Amy reached into her bra and removed her cell phone. Carefully she changed the phone settings from vibrate to silent and placed the phone in the bottom of her purse. She then pulled out a tissue to dry her eyes.

"Mom," she said reluctantly, "let's stop by the phone store on the way home. I think it's time to make a change and trade this phone in for a new model."

Amy paused a minute, and thinking aloud, continued, "And, Mom, maybe we can just make a quick stop at the Humane Society and see if there are any puppies that might be available."

DOT
"I hate to be called a widow!"

When Dot's husband died suddenly, she was lost. Dot and Tim had been a matched set for so long, she had no idea how, as a woman alone, she could bring her life back together again.

After struggling through a whirlwind of desperation, trying to fill this new void in her life, Dot finally discovers the secret. She'd been looking for love in all the wrong places.

Hi, I'm Dot, and I'm a widow!

This was Dot's introductory comment to me when we first met. In the early months after the sudden death of her husband, Tim, Dot functioned numbly-well, handling his funeral and taking care of the business of his death. Her adult children were proud of their Mom.

Much to her surprise and embarrassment, just months after Tim's funeral, Dot found herself spinning out of control. She was moving backward, and she was lost in a sea of confusion, isolation, and depression. In her own words, Dot tells her story.

WIDOW — For a long time, I felt as though that word was pasted across my back! I felt so vulnerable and lost and really hated the term. Widow? Isn't there a better expression for describing a woman whose husband has died?

Dot and Tim, that's what everyone called us. We had one name. We were a matched set, just like ice cream and cake, bacon and eggs, gin and vermouth. We were, or so we thought, the original "dynamic duo." We learned to fight fairly and we made up passionately. Tim and I married in college. Now I'm in my 60's. You do the math.

My parents always wanted me to "marry a nice religious boy," and I did. We shared our faith, and for years, we sat in the same pew every week at church. He was a salesman. I taught elementary school and loved being a teacher. It was the best of all worlds. I guess I should be grateful that Tim and I had so many good years together. Maybe I miss him even more because it was so good, most of the time.

Then, without warning Tim died. He was golfing with buddies. A heart attack. I wasn't there physically when he died, and I surely wasn't emotionally there during his funeral or for the first few years after his death.

Our two adult kids and their spouses flew in from out of state. We marched through the family funeral drill. I felt "mechanical," like a well-oiled machine. I drafted to-do lists for my son, daughter and for myself. The three of us split up the duties, making phone calls and arranging the funeral. We shared equally the dreadful experience of wandering around the 'casket selection room' to find the suitable 'container' for Dad. We drove over hill and dale in the local cemetery to find the right 'resting place.'

Looking back, during those days involving the funeral, I realized I'd behaved like a hostess at a reception. I wore a designer knit that I'd been saving 'for that special occasion.' How sad. I remember standing next to Tim's casket looking out over the line of people, all waiting to express their sympathy, hold my hand, touch my shoulder. They were shaking their heads in disbelief. I remember thinking about my shoes and wondering why did I wear these heels? My feet were killing me.

My mind raced, consumed with the to-do list of making endless phone calls, planning for the Mass and funeral followed by the graveside service, and picking up friends and relatives at the airport. I plastered on a smile and practiced my "Dot empathetic nod." And guess what? Dot-the-Robot made it through. Everyone was incredibly pleased with my performance.

ADRIFT — Feeling lost and alone

Then, my bravado and numbness began to slowly erode. I can't tell you when it happened, possibly after the first anniversary of Tim's death. The business of his death was over. Financial, insurance, and legal matters were settled. Now, I was suddenly adrift.

Like peeling the layers of an onion, my protective coat of disbelief began to fall away revealing the core of my grief. I hit a wall of complete immobility. He was not coming back. Tim was dead!

Sleep was never my friend. I'd toss and turn, walk the floor, get up, eat junk food, watch TV, go back to bed to hug my pillow and cry. I tried to make sleep friendly changes; snuggling on Tim's-side of the bed, moving the bedroom furniture all around my room. Nothing helped. I was resigned to forever seeing the dark raccoon circles under my eyes. Eating was insane; some weeks I would eat non-stop, others I would just nibble at food. I ate standing up at the kitchen counter, or on a sofa in front of the TV, or not at all. Preparing a normal meal and setting a place for just one person was unbearable.

I became completely disorganized! It wasn't unusual for me to find myself in the middle of the room and wonder what I was doing there, or to drive through an intersection unsure if the traffic light had been red or green. I was devoid of energy. Some days I wore my pajamas or sweats all day. Mail and bills piled up on the dining room table and I didn't care. Responding to messages took too much effort. The only appointments I kept were with my doctor. Seeing how depressed and disheveled I was, my internist suggested I take antidepressants. I dutifully accepted the prescription. But once I got home, I tossed it in the desk drawer.

Loneliness is a few steps below being alone! As an elementary school teacher, I recall grading a section dealing with students' socialization skills. The options were: (1) plays well with others or (2) plays well independently. If I were grading myself I was always the one who could play well with others, never independently. I was not used to being alone. I hated it. Oddly, almost simultaneously, I'd seek out and then avoid people. I found myself desperate for company, but even with friends I'd feel alone. I yearned for the security of home, but when I came back home I felt alone and lonely again.

My kids worried about me. Each one invited me to fly out to visit with them and their families. I dutifully accepted the invitations. Each trip I really tried to be "mom" for the visit, gluing myself together, pasting on the "Dot is fine smile." Each child delivered what I refer to as the kids' pep talk, suggesting I could find a job, or maybe sell my home and move in with them. I told them these weren't options for me. When I got back home, I felt worse than ever. Their lives were moving forward. Mine was going backward.

My daughter encouraged me to join what I called a "widowed ladies' group" in the community. I decided I'd force myself to go to a few meetings. Not caring how I looked, I showed up wearing a pair of sweats and tennis shoes. Before Tim died, I would never have been caught in public looking like this. The group offered speakers, small discussion groups, and outings. The members tried to be helpful, giving me friendly guidelines to "widowhood." Ugh! We talked about loss and grief and moving on. I could not fathom the moving on part. The only moving I was doing was deeper into a well of solitude.

PROMISCUITY — Looking for Love In All The Wrong Places

One constant in my life, and a thin one at that, was my religious faith. I tried to attend church regularly, although it felt strange sitting alone in what had, for so many years, been "our pew." One Sunday, the church bulletin announced a group for newly divorced and widowed men and women.

For some reason this didn't seem as overwhelming and depressing as the community widowed ladies club. In desperation, I started attending the new group at church, and forced myself to dress up for these meetings. "If I am going to try to meet new people I will do all I can to boost my ego as I walk in that door." I promised myself I would give it a fair trial and go at least three times.

The new group was informal, congenial and mixed. For the past two years, I had been interacting primarily with females. Listening to the men in the group, I realized how much I had missed the male perspective in my life. After several weeks, I found myself looking forward to the

Wednesday night meetings. I arrived early and stayed late; helping with coffee and meeting people. Social events were planned. I attended.

One man, Bob, also widowed, often sat next to me. Soon we began to meet for coffee, then for dinner. Before I realized it, Bob and I were dating. I loved having a man sitting with me in a restaurant and holding my hand as we walked. In less time than I would have anticipated, given my religious upbringing, I was having sex with Bob. It happened in his home. I couldn't take him to my home. I didn't love Bob, but I liked him enough to go to bed with him. Frankly, I didn't enjoy the sex, but I was hungry for closeness and holding. When we parted, I still felt isolated and lonely. This went on for several months. Each time I hoped Bob would fill the empty hole in my heart. I worried that I should feel guilty. What was I doing? This was certainly not the behavior of a nice Catholic girl.

I am also ashamed to admit that I started dating another man in the group. Hank, was divorced, younger, flashier and very exciting. Still hungry and desperate, I went out with him. We had sex; not love, but there was touching and warmth. Now I was balancing my "social life" between two men, neither of whom I loved. I just wanted to silence the scream of emptiness inside me.

I was in an emotional whirlwind, and felt like a teenager. In an effort to look more appealing, I joined a gym. This was a totally new experience for me. As I look back, I joined for all the wrong reasons. I did it to meet men, not to get healthy. I found myself flirting outrageously with strange men. This was not "Dot." My kids noticed a change in me. I now answered their phone calls and said I was "going out." Erroneously, they thought I was "getting better." They didn't realize their mother was becoming a promiscuous woman, and I couldn't tell them. I guess I didn't realize it either.

After seeing Dave at the gym for many weeks, he invited me out. I accepted immediately. How exciting, another new man in my life. As I was dressing for my date with Dave, I looked in the mirror, and I chided myself. Who is this man, Dave? I don't even know him! What am I doing? Running from myself? Suddenly I realized other men couldn't bring Tim back. They would never fill me up.

Who is Dot, anyway? I realized I had to take back responsibility for my life. I cancelled the date with Dave and took a leave from the singles group. I realized that by my standards, I'd been promiscuous. I was in chaos and I had created that chaos myself.

Making a Comeback

I found the name of a grief counselor and called for an appointment. I told her I was frightened, in trouble, and needed help finding my way back. That phone call was the first step in turning my life around.

Following that year of therapy I can look back and see how far I've come. I didn't realize, during the rough period of my grief, that I'd become a real mess. Therapy forced me to focus on my loneliness and resolve many issues. In my frenzy, somehow I'd decided a sexual partner was the answer to my loneliness. After several uncharacteristic flings with Bob, Hank and almost-Dave, I realized I was using those relationships to avoid dealing with my grief. The sex was a momentary relief, but it often left me feeling more alone and lonely than ever. Oh my!

It has now been five years since Tim's death. I've 'graduated' from therapy! I have new interests and many new friends, male and female. I'm open to meeting someone special, but certainly not 'playing around' as my kids call it. Yes, I still hate the term 'widow' and I do dislike living alone, but I'm having more good days than bad days. And best of all, I enjoy today and look forward to tomorrow.

BILL

"I've always been the 'family fixer'— but I can't fix my daughter's death"

Societal and cultural studies suggest particular behavioral patterns of men and women in grief. There are unwritten suggestions that women can cry and talk about their feelings and men should remain strong and in control. However, the emotions of loss show no gender preference. Regardless of how they both express grief, men and women can, and do, feel the overwhelming pain of loss.

Bill remembers his grief after his daughter's death and realizes that:

"Even grown up guys can cry!"

Bill — The Family Fixer

Around my house I was known as "the fixer." My wife or kids would ask: "Honey, can you fix the drip in the kitchen faucet?" or "Dad, the tire on my bike is flat. Can you fix it for me?" And I was thrilled to be in that role.

All that changed when my daughter, Susan, at age 18, died of bacterial meningitis. I was no longer the "family fixer." I couldn't fix anything, not my own grief or that of the rest of my family. I couldn't prevent her death and I couldn't bring her back. On top of my own incredible grief and loneliness, I felt I'd failed everyone else.

When I was growing up, there was a distinct difference between the particular roles men and women played in the family. A good husband was the protector. He provided for the family and did his best to keep "all the bad things away." While a wife could cry and show emotion, the husband should be strong and controlled. I prided myself on being that good, solid, protective husband and father.

None of that social conditioning protected me when it came to my grief. While my wife could cry, talk endlessly with friends, or just hit the couch with exhaustion; I felt I had to hold it all together. I envied her ability to "let it all out." I was more private and certainly hurting in ways others couldn't understand.

Colleagues at work would say, "Bill, you seem to be holding up well. We're sure proud of you!" What was I supposed to do with that? I wasn't holding up well at all. In fact, I was quietly disintegrating. I was so disappointed in myself. Where did that self sufficient, strong, independent guy go?

Looking back years later, I can see that I needed permission to grieve. All my male conditioning, all those expectations to "stand up on my own two feet and be counted," were only making things worse for me. Knowing what I know now, I wish I'd understand the value of really giving in to grief. "Giving in" doesn't interfere with the kind of guy we happened to be. In fact, I've realized over time, that some of the strongest men are the ones who are in touch with their emotions.

Yes, even grown up guys can cry!

Susan's death, and the grief that followed, changed my priorities. Many things, so critical to me before Susan's death, have little meaning today. Currently, my definition of a problem or a crisis is quite different. There's truth to the old expression "don't sweat the small stuff." Today the joy of success comes in personal ways, some times in baby steps. Now I find great joy in simpler things and smaller victories.

But it's been a long, tough journey and I struggled in many ways. For example, I think people who are dealing with grief become overwhelmed by questions others ask. Topics that are normal conversation for most people can be very difficult for a bereaved parent. Think of some of the following, seemingly innocent questions, such as:

HOW ARE YOU? People often ask that question out without thinking. Asking a grieving person, "How are you?" presents a problem. I'd think: "Well, now, if I told you how I REALLY am, you probably wouldn't hang around long." But out loud I'd say, "I'm OK."

HOW MANY CHILDREN DO YOU HAVE? This is a tough question for bereaved parents. The first few times that happened, I was stymied. If the situation were one where I could speak honestly, I'd respond: "Well, my wife Judy and I have three children. My middle child, Susan, died in her Freshman year of college. I also have an older daughter, Marianne, and a younger son, David." That way, I included Susan, but didn't make the other person feel too uncomfortable. It's hard to answer the question in a different way because you feel you are dismissing your dead child.

However, at work, when I wasn't comfortable getting into an emotional discussion of my daughter's death, I would respond with what I hoped would change the subject: "I have two children, Marianne and David. Please, tell me about YOUR family?" That was my way of moving the focus from my situation and talking about their family. While that helped avoid an emotional discussion, it made me feel awful every time I said it. How could I omit my daughter Susan from the discussion?

HOW LONG DOES GRIEF TAKE? I interpreted this question as a signal to me, "Isn't it time you moved on?" Grief takes such a long time. I'm an engineer-type-guy. I like to know how things work. I like to predict things that have a beginning, a middle, and an end. But, grief defies all order. Here I was, up and down, in and out, and all over the place. That complicated things for me.

Speaking of the "timing of grief," I was encouraged by others to find "closure." Closure implies a conclusion, and ending, a finalization, but there was no closure for me. The frustrating reality was that I couldn't close it off with a nice, tight seal. For me grief seemed to go on endlessly.

DO MEN GRIEVE DIFFERENTLY THAN WOMEN? Grief is such a personal, private experience. I felt isolated in my grief. Internally, I struggled with the feeling that somehow I had let my daughter down. I know her death was out of my control, but I still constantly wrestled with the image of being the family protector, the man of the house who ensures the safety of others.

As men, we lack the social permission to talk about more personal, sensitive issues. Culturally, it's easier for women to get together and talk. But not for men, even though we both suffer equally from broken hearts.

Dealing with his grief was a long process for Bill. He wrote a summary of his own ideas that helped him through the process. He titled his ideas "TAKING STEPS."

Taking Steps

SOCIAL OUTINGS — One of my first social outings was going to a hockey game with some buddies about two months after Susan's funeral. I love hockey. There I was with good friends, great seats and it was a good game, but all the time I was there I felt guilty. I sat there thinking:

"I'm crying inside. This isn't right, I shouldn't be here!" I wondered then, how I could ever laugh or have a good time again?

KILLING THE PAIN — For many guys, I know there's a temptation to mitigate pain with alcohol or abuse prescription drugs. The relief I tried was with alcohol. While it works in one way (you feel less pain), it also comes back to you with deeper depression. I know it's tempting. It's legal, accessible and socially acceptable. While the thought that Susan was gone never left me, I realized the quick fix of alcohol wasn't the answer.

BEREAVED PARENT SUPPORT GROUP — Following Susan's death, my wife and I attended a bereaved parent support group sponsored by a local hospital. At the beginning of the meetings, everyone in the room introduced themselves and shared their story. They told the name of their child and how the death happened. In some ways the group did help. I finally realized we weren't the only grieving parents in the world. Nothing could bring Susan back to us, but there was comfort in seeing other bereaved parents walking and talking and living their lives.

BACK TO WORK — Returning to work after Susan's funeral was a challenge, but it was good for me to be there. On the job, I needed to function, walk, talk and make decisions. I was forced to use my mind and creativity. Returning to work also brought added challenges. My colleagues didn't really know what to say to me or whether or not to mention Susan. I found that the ball was in my court. I was in the unenviable position of either giving others permission to talk about my daughter by bringing up something about Susan, or of changing the subject and returning to a work-as-usual mode. Most of the time I felt I was carefully holding myself together and I couldn't afford to lose my public face. I focused on the work-as-usual mode.

DOWN TIME — Keeping busy helped. It was not that I was forgetting Susan or my grief. But I was living with imposed structure, putting one foot in front of another, and that was helpful. I told my wife that on weekdays I was "functional," but on weekends, I was "non-functional." Weekends were the most difficult for me.

COMFORT AND ANGER IN FAITH — While faith is an integral part of my life, I found myself wondering how could God let this happen to our family? God is our protector, isn't He? For that matter, how could I, as a protector, let this happen to my family? One of my friends suggested that God could handle my anger. I was an usher at church, and I honored my commitment of being there weekly. Being in church forced me to be alone with my feelings. Sometimes I'd be swallowing tears, but I at least was there. I felt good about that part.

I feel fortunate to have faith. I don't think "faith" always means we must worship at synagogue, church, or mosque. I think it is something deep in our heart, regardless of how we manifest it. I confess it helps me feel Susan "is there."

MEMORIES THAT CONNECT ME TO SUSAN — A Priest, Father Tom Slowinski, has said that "Memory is the cradle of love." I completely agree with him. Memories of Susan keep her close to me. Telling Susan-stories and having photos and objects that connect me to Susan, brings me great comfort. My wife and I had put pictures of Susan in a big box, but for a very long time, I couldn't convince myself to get that box out. When I finally had the courage to open the box, while it was with great pain that I looked at the pictures, it was also very comforting.

Small things really made a difference. Susan's clothes, music tapes, and personal objects became very important. Not long after her funeral, one of our cars was stolen. Insurance covered the financial value of the car, but what bothered me most about the incident was that her college parking sticker (WMU) was on the window. It felt like an invasion of my connection to her — somebody stealing her college parking sticker. I could replace the car but not her parking sticker.

Bitter or Better

I didn't want to be immobilized by my grief. After a certain point, I needed to try to move forward. I'd heard the expression, "bitter or better," and decided I didn't want to be labeled as a bitter person. This wasn't a sudden epiphany; it was a gradual thing that evolved. But once I'd come to terms with that concept, slowly the days did become better.

It's amazing to me to realize how much my priorities have changed. I think about things so differently, including the way I spend my time. For example, I give my time to other people in grief. I'm involved in a parish bereavement program where I make myself available to other bereaved parents. When mutually bereaved parents speak with one another, there's a strong bond. They know we are very sincere when we ask them, "How are you really doing?"

I've learned there are no magic words to say to another in grief. However, having confronted a major loss, I've gained a quiet perspective about helping another. Sometimes just giving another dad a knowing nod, a smile, or a hand on the shoulder can speak volumes. Those of us who survive this kind of loss have a silent bond that is very powerful and helpful.

These are all gifts I have gained as a result of my grief. I've turned a corner. I can clearly say that finally the pressure is now off. I'm no longer the "Family Fixer." Now I'm just Dad.

SHANNON

"MY DAUGHTER'S ROADSIDE MEMORIAL WAS A WAY TO CARE FOR HER AFTER HER FUNERAL"

The funeral for her 16-year old daughter had ended, but Kay felt her grief had barely begun. She was still in a state of shock and disbelief over such an unexpected loss.

Then she created a special place to express her grief. Shannon's Roadside Memorial became a meaningful place where loved ones could come together to try to find reality in an unreal situation and share their love for this vivacious, much loved teenager.

A Mother's Grief and a Roadside Memorial

It was my friend, Kay, who opened my eyes to the personal significance of roadside memorials. For some time I've seen these memorials along highways, in fields, on bridge abutments, and near intersections. If I'm driving too fast, they are a sharp warning to me, to slow down and drive more carefully. Sometimes, driving along, I've looked at them with a mixture of sadness and curiosity, feeling badly that someone died at that spot, and wondering how it happened. At other times, (before Kay enlightened me about their significance) if I'd been having a particularly good day, I'd quickly look away, not wanting to think about the sadness of what must have happened there, and even feel annoyed, as though the harsh reminder of such sadness kind of ruined my day.

Kay's daughter, Shannon, died in a car crash along a two-lane country road. After her funeral, Kay struggled with her deep need to continue caring for her daughter. What could she do? Her answer came when she decided to erect a roadside memorial at the site of Shannon's death.

On each anniversary of her death, Kay observes her own ritual. She revisits the memorial and lights a candle for each year that has passed since Shannon died. When I asked her about it, Kay said these small rituals are important because sometimes actions can speak when words fail. She calls the rituals her "walking sticks" to help her get down the long road of grief.

On the fourth year after Shannon's death, Kay invited me to join her in her memorial candle lighting ritual. I accepted. I had never met her daughter, but on that warm August evening, I was introduced to Shannon through her mother's story.

It was dusk, the time of day in late summer in Northern Michigan when trees become veiled silhouettes against the crimson sky. We rode in silence. Kay carefully maneuvered her car along the wooded country roads leading to Shannon's memorial. For some reason, riding along, I thought of a verse from a poem I'd learned years ago called "The Children's Hour," by H. D. Longfellow: "Between the dark and the daylight, when the night is beginning to lower, comes a pause in the day's occupations, that is known as the Children's Hour." Riding along, I was aware that this was that particular time of day — "the children's hour."

The Wounds of Nature Heal Slowly!

We were on a narrow two lane road. As we rounded a sharp turn I saw to my left, a simple wooden cross, erected slightly back off the road.

Kay pulled over to the easement to park her car, and we got out. We each found a place to sit, quietly settling into the tall wild grasses near the cross. On and around the cross were tiny pieces of windshield glass, trinkets, beads, shining stones, stuffed animals, photos, and hand written notes addressed to Shannon.

Beyond the memorial, I could still see the remnants of the path that Shannon's car cut through the woods that night. Her path had dead-ended as her Chrysler Le Baron had struck a huge tree and landed upside down. I could still see how the impact of Shannon's car inflicted deep gashes and wounds in the trunk of the tree. It was so hard to believe such tragedy could occur in this quiet, peaceful wooded area.

I inhaled the deep pine smell of the forest and listened to the night sounds as animals began to speak in their evening language. Looking down into the grasses, I noticed a tiny piece of shining metal, perhaps from Shannon's headlight. Impulsively I picked it up. Fingering the piece of metal, I wondered how many years these buried pieces of Shannon's car would continue to find their way to surface of the earth.

Meeting Shannon

Silently Kay arranged four candles in a metal stand. She lit them one by one. Then she sat back down next to me in the tall grasses. The light from the candles illuminated her face, highlighting the tears running down her cheeks. Kay removed her glasses, rubbed her eyes, and began to tell the story. She brought me back with her to a night four years earlier, and introduced me to her daughter. "If ever there was a teenager who grabbed every nibble of life, it was Shannon," Kay said, smiling at the memory.

"She was 16 that summer, and had her driver's license. Shannon, her younger brother, Aaron, and I were enjoying our annual vacation in Northern Michigan. She loved being up North and now she had a maroon Chrysler Le Baron, which she drove with the windows down so she could let her hair blow. Shannon was drawn to the curving, challenging back woods roads that led to exciting places and great friends."

Kay leaned over to blow out the candles: "Shannon always had a wild and restless spirit, but she was also very responsible. She always got home on time, or called to let me know she'd be late. So, on this particular night when she was late getting home, I began to worry. It wasn't like her to not check in, so I called the friend she'd been visiting. I was told Shannon 'had left a while ago.' Now, remember," Kay paused, "this was before everyone carried a cell phone, so communication was not as instantaneous."

"My gut told me something was wrong. I grabbed my car keys and immediately started driving the roads Shannon would have to take to get home. Because I'd left immediately, I missed the subsequent phone call telling me that two of Shannon's friends had also started looking for her car.

In reality, they were not only looking for Shannon, they had already found her! They discovered she'd had an accident on one of the back roads, and had run to a neighboring farm to call 911."

I was listening to Kay's story so intently, I didn't realize that it was now dark and stars were shining above us. Kay fingered her glasses in her lap. Finally she spoke again: "I don't know how long I drove around looking for her. All I know is I was rounding the curve on this road and I abruptly came upon the scene of the accident. I yanked my car off the road, and ran to the site. My heart stopped! I couldn't see Shannon, but I could see where her car had completely missed the curve and careened off into the woods."

Shaking her head, her eyes closed, Kay continued: "The 911 teams arrived before I even found my daughter! I pulled up to the scene and flashing lights were blinding my eyes. Police and rescue teams, including the Medical Examiner, were already there. Oh God, the sounds — sirens wailing, people yelling — I'll never forget them. I ran past the workers and stared down the embankment. There it was. Shannon's car. She had missed the curve, hit a tree and landed upside down."

"As I'm reliving this," Kay looked directly into my eyes, " I'm amazed at how quickly rescue teams responded. I'm her mother, and they got there before me. It was so horrible to come upon that scene. The 'jaws of life' had already arrived at the scene. I stood there in shock, listening to the angry, grinding sounds that machine made as it was tearing at Shannon's car. The machine had to rip it apart to get her out of the front seat."

Shannon's Beautiful, Wild, and Restless Spirit was Forever Silenced

Kay described the days following Shannon's death as a blur. They were filled with decisions about choices, some unreal and others unimaginable. Who will notify family and friends? Who's a good funeral director? What kind of funeral should we have? Where do you bury your 16 year old?

Shaking her head and raising her hand as if to say "halt," Kay said: "It was all happening so fast! Shannon died. No preparation. She just died.

Then, of course, we had to have a funeral. I just wanted everything to slow down so I could catch up. It was unbelievable."

Kay said she moved on autopilot, checking off items from a never-ending list. She returned endless phone calls, made funeral arrangements, found a place for her daughter at a cemetery, and numbly met the sea of people who came to Shannon's funeral.

The knot in her throat began to feel permanent and the overwhelming feeling of "This can't be happening to me," was ever-present. "Even when I was surrounded by people," Kay said, "I felt alone."

What Does a Mom do After the Funeral of her Child?

"The funeral was over," Kay explained, "but I needed to do something, anything, to try to find reality in this unreal situation. Since the day she was born I had taken care of Shannon. For 16 years, 7 months and 4 days I had 'done things' for her. Suddenly there was nothing left to do for her anymore. Going to the cemetery was not enough. I needed to be at the place where she died, not at the place where she was buried. That's when I decided to create a roadside memorial for her. It gave me something tangible to do for her — and for me."

Kay was comparing the cemetery with the place Shannon died: "Creating the roadside memorial, where Shannon lost control of her car, was creating a sense of reality for me. I didn't have that feeling at the funeral home or the cemetery. By creating her memorial, at the curve of the road, Shannon's death became real, and I believe reality helps us heal. If we find some sense of reality in a situation, and we can really feel it, (even if it's the acute pain of loss), we can heal it. What I'm trying to say is you can't heal what you can't feel."

"Creating the roadside memorial with the large, simple wooden cross," Kay went on to explain, "gave us a place where we could bring tokens and pieces of our lives to leave with her. It was a way of still touching Shannon long after her funeral. I think her relatives and friends felt as numb as I did at the funeral. Here, at the roadside memorial, we can gather, hold one another, cry, and remember in a way we couldn't at the funeral or the cemetery."

Kay summed it up best when she reflected: "This is the place where all control was lost. By 'all control' I mean control in Shannon's life and in mine. It is the place where I lost my daughter. It is the place where I hope to find myself again."

After many years she continues to care for the site. "I use a hand trimmer to cut back the weeds and tall grasses. It's labor intensive, maybe like penitence. I plant flowers and bring things that I wish I could give to Shannon. I want to express in death what I can no longer express in life."

Why do Grieving People Create these Roadside Memorials?

My experience with Kay that night helped me better understand the meaning of a roadside memorial. The place where the death occurred has great significance to loved ones. I now also understand how, when it's possible, families whose loved ones die in military service or in accidents far from home, feel compelled to go to the place where their loved one died. Some travel long distances, to remote battlefields and far away places. They want to stand on the ground where their child, spouse, parent, sibling or lover last stood. In a very personal way, it seems to bring reality to their loss.

Today roadside memorials are found around the world; along roadsides of places as diverse as sharp edges of cliffs in Greece, to interstate highways and dusty rural country roads. Some roadside memorials are simple and crude, such as two boards nailed together to form a cross, or a gnarled metal object nailed to a tree. Others are more elaborate with intricate markings, sculpture, photographs, trinkets, and pieces of twisted metal from a motorcycle or car, artificial flowers, stuffed animals, and flags.

All are expressions of love and symbols of the life that was lost at that place.

A Final Thought

When I see a memorial along a road and it's possible to stop, I try to pull over to pay my respect to the families involved in such accidents. One day when I had stopped at such a memorial near a field, another driver was also standing there. He was looking at it and shaking his head in a negative fashion.

I was standing there silently when he looked at me and said: "I don't get it. What is it with these things along the road? They're traffic hazards. They really bug me. I just can't see why these people can't confine this behavior to the cemetery."

I shook my head. Feeling it was something we just have to experience, I didn't think I could explain it to him no matter how I tried.

After my personal experience with Kay and Shannon's roadside memorial I now "get it." I clearly understand what they mean to the survivors of the loss and why they are important.

Roadside memorials are an extension and visible expression of grief. They are a timeless testimony to the cycles of life and death and to the concept that reality promotes healing.

Shannon's Roadside Memorial / by Michael Dean Gilbert

Kay wrote the following poem 16 years after Shannon's death.

PRAISE GRIEF
For The Lessons I Have Learned When Bent To My Knees By Her Presence

That may seem strange; to praise grief, but it isn't strange for me.
I have had to learn to live with grief for it will always be a part of me.
I accept this as my reality.
Grief has woven an intricate pattern into the very fabric of my life.
I respect grief and give her space
But I no longer allow her to define my life.

I have had to accept that now, with very few exceptions,
The people in my life
Did not even know me at the time of Shannon's death.
With her death it was as if I became a star grown dim
No longer visible to the people in my life.

Death has shown me the value of life and
How precious and fragile it is.
Death has opened my eyes to the joys of life.
Death has reminded me never to miss a sunrise.
Death has offered me hands to hold,
Hugs to give, people to love.
Death has made me a more compassionate person,
A kinder, gentler soul.

For me, grief and the death from which it was born
Was the ultimate destroyer of my beliefs and dreams.
Left in the wake of the destruction was a
Hollow, empty shell of myself,
Buried beneath mounds of ash and rubble.

But rubble and ash
Proved to be a good breeding ground
For thoughts and ideas.
It gave rise to growth
And a quest for new truths.

I praise grief
For the lessons
I have learned
When bent to my knees
By her presence.

- Kay L. Sturgeon

CHUCK

"My doctor tells me these physical problems are related to unresolved grief"

Delayed Grief

I answered my telephone to a strong, masculine voice, speaking clearly and succinctly: "Doctor, my name is Chuck. I'm having some health problems, and apparently my medical doctor thinks they're related to grief. He directed me to you."

He paused to take a short breath and announced: "I've never asked for help before. I'm a pretty self-sufficient guy. But, this grief stuff — I'm completely lost here! When can we schedule an appointment?"

In our first meeting, I noticed he was a casually dressed man, with close cropped hair and ramrod straight posture. He nodded politely and shook my hand firmly. Without hesitation, he walked directly to the couch and sat down. "Where do we begin?"

"Well, Chuck, tell me about yourself," I answered. "Why are you here today?"

Chuck began his report: "I can't eat, can't sleep, my heart races and my blood pressure's off the charts. I've never been anxious or depressed, but right now I am all of that and more. My internist put me on medication. He told me I'm flirting with serious health problems, and suggested I get help with this. All this therapy business is a first for me."

Chuck stopped and spread his hands out to each side as if asking, "Should I go on?"

"Please continue," I said.

"Two years ago, my wife, Andrea, died unexpectedly of a heart attack. I always thought it was the men who had heart attacks."

"I was totally unprepared. Andrea died without warning. Losing her was a shock," he stopped for a moment remembering, then went on: "It was rough, but at the time I thought I handled it pretty well. I notified everyone, and then I arranged her funeral and burial. I also tried to help our son, Chad, get through it. Chad's in his 20's. Actually, he's Charles III. He's a good kid."

He paused, collecting his thoughts: "Doctor, I don't think I shed a tear after her funeral. I threw myself into my business. That's how I handle things, you know. I get busy and keep moving." Chuck gestured with his hands, lifting fingers to point out his list: "I have maintained my daily routine; up early, quick breakfast and then I'm off to the gym. I spend roughly eight to ten hours at the office. Until recently, every evening, like a good son, I would visit my Dad. He was struggling with prostate cancer. He and I spent a lot of time together." Chuck was nodding his head in an affirmative gesture. " I took great care of Dad, right up to the day he died — just three months ago."

It's All Catching Up with Me

I asked Chuck to tell me more about his philosophy of "get busy and keep moving."

He leaned forward on the couch: "Well, do you know the term 'a man's man?' That would be the men of our family; my Dad, myself, my son. We're all named Charles and we're all military men. Dad was in World War II, I'm a veteran of Vietnam, and Chad is active duty, recently deployed to Iraq. I guess you could say we're a disciplined bunch. I don't know another way to explain it. Our slogan is: 'Whatever happens — just handle it!'"

Suddenly Chuck was quiet. He looked away from me, directing his eyes to a painting on the wall. After allowing a little breathing time, I broke the silence: "Chuck, what were you thinking about just now?"

When he spoke again, his voice had lost its authoritative tone: "It's just that as I'm telling you all this it seems like so much! Yet people deal with a lot worse kinds of situations. My Dad's death was rough, but he was 87. That's a nice long life!"

"Andrea was only 56 when she died," Chuck leaned back into the couch, relaxing his posture. "Even though I really miss my Dad, I have to think his death, after a long illness, is different from Andrea's sudden death. I still miss her every day, but it was two years ago. Two years! Doesn't it seem as though I should be over it by now?"

I took my time answering: "I don't think grief has a time table. I do know it takes a long time. And, grief is patient. It waits for us, Chuck. Keeping busy helps keep grief at bay, but it doesn't make the sadness go away."

"You've got that right, Doctor," he said. "I guess it's all catching up with me now. I'm afraid to slow down; and I'm afraid not to! Does that make sense?"

"Yes, yes it does." I agreed.

Chuck forged ahead: " In my last physical, my doctor was shocked at my 'numbers' — heart rate, blood pressure, weight loss. He says it's all stress and grief; that I need to take a look at those things — whatever that means. That's why I'm here."

I asked about his son in the service. "Chad was deployed to Iraq nine months ago," Chuck said. "I've always known the deal with overseas deployment. It's a real waiting game. You talk about 'grief being patient.' When your kid is overseas, as a parent you really have to be patient. You hear from him only when he can get word out and you shouldn't let yourself worry about it. Up until now, I've handled it OK."

Chuck shook his head: "Now I worry constantly. Since Dad died, I can't stop obsessing about my son dying over there. I'm glued to my cell phone and my computer, waiting to hear from him. I have nightmares about Chad being captured and tortured. Not only that, now I'm having bad dreams about Andrea. I obsess about everything. I wonder, should I have known about her bad heart? Was I a good husband to her? Have I let my family down somehow? These are the kinds of things that go through my mind all the time, Doctor."

Squaring his shoulders, Chuck said: "So, now my wife and Dad are dead and my son is in Iraq. I can't believe it! Even our damned 10-year-old dog just died." Chuck allowed a glimmer of a smile: "We called the dog 'Patriot.' a fitting name for our family I guess. I sure do miss that mutt greeting me at the door. Patriot dying was just another nail in the coffin, so to speak."

Chuck leaned back against the couch, almost in a sign of silent resignation: " I've always considered myself a strong guy, carrying on no matter what. Now I'm like a lost puppy! Keeping busy isn't working for me anymore. I've never asked for help before, but the truth is I'm looking for guidance before this gets worse."

He asked directly: " So tell me, Doc, how long do you think this will take?"

Pealing Back the Layers

I thought it through in my mind. To help Chuck get to the root of the problem, we had to gradually pull back the layers of his grief; beginning with his hyperactivity and his denial. Chuck would have to slow down, redirect his overdrive, and stop running from emotion. This would be difficult as Chuck was used to having control over his emotions and be-haviors. He'd have to consider allowing himself to feel the emotions he had struggled to suppress.

"Let's look at it this way, Chuck," I suggested. "You have a lot on your plate. Let's tackle this one step at a time. Your health is compromised and you've seen your physician. He sent you to me. Those are two big steps for you. I think you should feel good about that."

He nodded affirmatively and I continued: "Together we can sort this out. Of the many things you're worried about, let's look at what you have control over and what you can change in your life."

Chuck was listening and I continued: "Right now, your son's fate is out of your control, but of course you remain available to communicate when it's possible. That does give you some control. Recently, your dog, Patriot, just died, and while he had a good 10 years, it's still tough because no pooch is wagging his tail to greet you at the door after work."

Chuck gave me a knowing smile when I mentioned his dog Patriot.

I continued with the difficulties of his grief: "Chuck, it's completely understandable to still be dealing with the unexpected death of your wife two years ago. You had no preparation in your loss of Andrea. And while you weren't surprised about your Dad's death months ago, it's a major loss. I suspect you even miss the companionship and care giving role you had with your Dad."

Chuck nodded in agreement: "I do, I do."

We continued to explore a new direction. "Chuck, all aspects of your life have changed," I noted. "Everybody's gone. You feel vulnerable. And now you've added another layer of grief; anticipatory grief — worry and fear for your son. Chad's fighting a war in Iraq, and you have no control over helping him or even knowing when you'll hear from him. As your internist suggested, perhaps the stress and grief are causing your physical problems. What has happened in your life is a lot to put on one man's shoulders."

"I hadn't thought about it that way. You're right, that it's a lot to deal with." Chuck was listening carefully.

"It is, yes it is," I agreed. "Andrea died two years ago. I think you miss her very much. It may help, and sometimes it is necessary, to back up and grieve for her as you might have two years ago. Chuck, remember, there is no time limit on grief. It's OK. Take all the time you need."

My last few words seemed to resonate with Chuck. He sat back more comfortably. His face looked more relaxed. He was nodding affirmatively and said: "You said no time limit on this? That helps. When my internist suggested I come here, I was worried that maybe I'd really lost my grip. OK, I understand. I'll keep coming until we get this thing resolved!"

Regaining Control

Chuck had lived the "man of action" approach to life. That was his natural way and familiar to him. He knew how to manage his life this way. He thought he could control his grief as he controlled his life, but now changes were necessary. Together we worked toward the realization that he'd already taken action and initiated the first two important steps; consulting a medical doctor and exploring grief therapy. Finally, he was on his way to envisioning a healthier future.

CHAPTER FIVE

Late Grief

THE RESOLUTION

"WE BEGIN TO THINK OF A POSSIBLE FUTURE,
WITH NEW HILLS TO CLIMB AND
NEW SIGHTS TO SEE"

"When we are no longer able to change a situation —
we are challenged to change ourselves"

- Viktor Frankl

Coming to Terms with Loss

Grief is a long journey, an important period of life that ironically "begins with an end." When we are lost in the wilderness of grief, it's difficult to imagine that it will ever end. We just want 'the good old days' to return! While the good old days won't return, there are new days ahead, and over time most of us are ready to enter the final phase of healing which I call Late Grief — The Resolution.

In this Resolution phase of Late Grief we begin to consider new beginnings, new ideas, and even new chapters in life. Changes can be subtle. We don't just awaken one day and feel better. We realize that we don't heal from grief, as we would a cold or the flu. But, we do resolve it. We grow within and beyond it.

It's not unusual, from time to time, to slide back into the throes of sadness. However, the overall tenor of life now becomes more positive and hopeful. We start to feel better both physically and emotionally. Energy returns and we find ourselves wanting to become more involved in a life beyond our grief. As we start changing our priorities, we begin to understand and accept our loss.

The funeral for Jan's daughter, Lindsay, had taken place almost two years previously when Jan confessed: "There was a time when I couldn't remember the sound of Lindsay's voice! I even had trouble remembering the real 'me!' Now that I am feeling better and seem to have turned a corner, I find Lindsay is a part of me in a whole new, special way. Now I can hear her laugh and even remember her voice. I see Lindsay in so many other children, and I realize I'm beginning to feel so much better!"

In Late Grief, we worry about forgetting that special person who died, only to discover we don't need to talk about our loved one as much because we've incorporated him or her in our lives in a new way. Yet the ambiguity is confusing. At first it may feel contrary. "Feeling better" may feel abnormal or wrong somehow. While we begin again to find some joy and happiness in everyday life, we may also fear that "we are leaving our loved one behind."

As our healing continues and we resolve our loss, we also realize that we have brought our loved one into our lives in a new, deeper way. Robert realized this when he received a long-awaited promotion at work.

"I was given a big corporate reward, and a huge raise," he remembered. "Somehow at that moment, even though he died three years ago, I just knew my Dad would've been so proud of me. I always wanted his approval and at that moment, I knew I had it. I had moved Dad into a deeper place in my heart."

Glen is an admitted lover of Country Music. When talking about his grief after the death of his son, he remembered: "There's a country song that has the phrase 'I've been DOWN so long, it looks like UP to me.' That was just how I felt for a few years. I just couldn't imagine ever feeling 'up' again. Then I worried that somehow, if I did begin to 'feel better,' I'd forget my son. But I am gradually feeling 'up' again and my memories of my son are brighter than ever. I can see now this whole experience has made me a better guy. I understand so much more now."

Gradually, as we begin to emerge from the depth of our experience, we realize it's OK to take charge of our lives and move on. And there's good news ahead. We start to feel better both physically and emotionally.

We can now reach out, make changes, and even enjoy life again. This brings a sense of freedom. Slowly we can begin again to make plans for the future and to move beyond the loss, which dominated our lives for so long.

In Late Grief we learn to honor our memories and realize there are new discoveries and joys ahead.

The five stories in this chapter on Late Grief describe the resolution of particular losses. These stories remind us of the many ways we can incorporate a loved one into our everyday life and of the often unexpected growth and understanding we realize as we move forward.

The haunting echoes of September 11, 2001, known world-wide as "9/11," continue to remind Maria of where she was and exactly what she was doing in New York City's financial district on that fateful day. An unexpected loud backfire of an engine, the smell of burning rubber, or the sight of a man in a red necktie immediately take Maria back to 9/11.

Kay, a young widow at 39, and Shellee, her teenage daughter, each react in a different way when their husband and father, Jerry, dies. Just as they follow one another in life, so do the stories follow one another; first of Kay, a newly widowed mother, then Shellee, her young daughter. Each shares the personal challenge of adjusting to life without Jerry, the family hero.

Jim struggles for some time with the deaths of first, his father, then his mother. Dealing with the cognitive and business aspects of his loss is much easier than the emotional uncertainty. Eventually, he comes to terms with his experience through a most unexpected event.

Margaret and Earl had enjoyed so many years together, they often found themselves finishing one another's sentences. Margaret brings us along on her journey of remembered joy as she deals with the loss of her lifelong love.

MARIA

"After all these years, the echoes of 9/11 still haunt me!"

The Echoes of 9/11

The 9/11 attacks on New York City took less than two hours. Yet the impact remains for years, as survivors continue to try to resolve the emotional injuries of that fateful day.

The experiences of those who survived that traumatic day resonated throughout the world. It also left countless survivors changed in ways that are difficult to measure. What does intense trauma do to us? When we see damage, loss, and death all around us, what is the long-term effect of such an experience? What kind of prolonged grief do we experience? How does grief affect us in the years following the traumatic event?

Trauma survivors often experience a form of prolonged grief. Memories of the experience resurface periodically, sending them back into an emotional turmoil. Maria, a New York resident and survivor, describes how the memories continue to haunt her.

On the morning of 9/11, Maria was busy working at her desk in down-town New York City. Although many years have passed, she remembers that day with deep emotion. Stimuli such as a burning odor, the beeping sound of an emergency vehicle, or a man wearing a red necktie, immediately send Maria back to that morning when she found herself running ankle-deep in gray ash to escape the assailants who were attacking her city.

Maria Tells her Story with a Continued Sense of Passion and Grief

I worked on the 17th floor of a building on Broadway, near the World Trade Center. It was early morning and all of us in the office were beginning our workday. The hum of the office was interrupted by a horrible noise.

Without warning the first plane hit the Trade Center. Everyone in the office rushed to the windows, looking up at a fire, high in the sky toward the top part of the North Tower. At first we thought a small plane or helicopter had accidentally hit the Tower. We stared, mesmerized at the gaping hole and the billowing clouds of black smoke.

Suddenly I saw something tumbling down, and heard someone shout: 'Oh my God!' I focused on what I thought was debris falling. It was a man tumbling downward toward the ground. The man must've jumped out a window to avoid burning to death. I could see he was wearing a red tie, and the tie was parachuting over his shoulder. Horrified, I instantly turned away. That poor man! I still can't get that awful sight out of my head.

Then our building shook. I held onto the desk as I watched the fireball of the second plane tear a huge hole through the South Tower. 'Good Lord, what's going on?' I thought to myself.

A shout went up: 'Let's get out of here!' We started to run, pushing through the emergency door toward the stairs. We were 17 flights up from the first floor, and we started down the winding stair, crushing, pushing, around and around, down and down. My arms were numb. I could hardly breathe. I was operating on autopilot.

Nothing made sense.

A Spiral Stairwell Banister Gripped by Frantic Hands

Abruptly we stopped! The frantic herd of people, desperate to get to the main floor and exit the building, had come to an unexpected halt. I looked down through the middle of the winding staircase and as far as I could see, there were hands tightly knotted together, gripping the metal circular banisters, creating a spiral pattern all the way down. Voices came from all around me. 'Why aren't we moving?' 'What's going on?' 'We've got to get out of here!'

Someone began shouting for quiet, so we could hear instructions from below. Word came up that there were so many rescue workers in front of the building that we wouldn't be able to get out. So we 'had to be patient.'

Time passed. It was so hot! I desperately tried to calm myself, but my fear and anxiety won. There was no way I could be calm or patient. Then the stairway began to fill with ash. People around me started to panic, thinking it was smoke. We were told to leave the stairwell immediately and enter the floor we were closest to.

I entered the seventh floor. I just stood there leaning against a wall, trying to catch my breath. I didn't know what was filling the stairs. *Was it smoke? Where was the fire? Would our building be the next one hit? Is this the day I would die?* I just didn't know. My mind was racing a thousand miles an hour.

Finally, a group of us found our way to the building's central computer room on the second floor. Rescue workers were still blocking our exit, so for the next two and a half hours we stayed in that room. Every 15 minutes an announcement came over the public address system, directing us to stay inside. It appeared to be the safest place at that time.

Some people, frantic to escape, ran back out into the stairwell, down to the main floor and then out toward the street. They quickly returned with bloodshot eyes, covered in gray ash from head to toe.

At around one o'clock, we were finally told it was safe to continue forward. They reassured us that we'd be given wet washcloths to cover our faces.

Once we exited the building, the plan was to walk across the Brooklyn Bridge.

Shocking Disbelief — A Fierce Snowstorm of Fallen Ash

I kept working my way toward the revolving doors on the main floor. I could see pieces of mangled metal, chunks of marble, and shattered glass. As we approached the exit I could finally see outside.

It looked just like a fierce horizontal snowstorm! Only it wasn't snow, it was falling ash. Through the debris, I could see hundreds of police and firemen standing in a line, all looking up in silent disbelief.

Everyone was staring up into the abyss, and I did too — until my eyes began to burn and I had to look away. In the distance, thousands of people were walking across the Brooklyn Bridge. The police were hurrying us along, directing us away from the scene.

There were shreds of paper flying everywhere through the air. It was then that I realized I was walking up to my ankles in the ash which coated the sidewalks and streets. I was part of the crowd moving toward the bridge.

It's odd the things you remember. Everyone walking across the bridge seemed to be dazed and exhausted. As I finally approached the bridge, my right foot began to cramp. I took off my shoe so I could continue walking. Now my foot began to hurt from walking barefoot.

It seemed to take forever to cross the bridge that day. I remember thinking: 'This is NOT happening!' But it was happening. It did happen. And I escaped with my life!

I felt numb for a long time after 9/11. Somebody could bump into me on the street and I wouldn't flinch. I had terrible dreams. They were more like nightmares; hearing low flying planes and seeing explosions. After the initial shock and numbness wore off, I realized I was on hyper-alert. Everything startled me, I'd break out in a sweat, my heart would race and I had anxiety most of the time. I grieved for friends, complete strangers, and for our city. I felt guilty. I survived! I made it, but so many others died.

Over time, there were many stories of the 9/11 exodus; of thousands of people rushing north and away from Ground Zero. There were stories of many random acts of kindness. We shared stories of the kind and good things that happened in the midst of tragedy. I heard of shopkeepers, randomly handing out bottles of water to those passing by. My friend's fiancée, who is blind, walked 25 miles, gripping the elbow of a stranger who led him to safety. His feet were bleeding by the time the ordeal was over, but thanks to a total stranger — he was safe.

I also learned that 'my man in the red necktie' (as I call him) was only one of the many who jumped from the burning building. People jumped through windows already broken, and some they broke themselves.

Those horribly frightened people were streaming down from all four sides of the burning building that whole time before the North Tower fell.

As I look back, even after all this time, it's startling how I continue re-living certain things. The sights, sounds and smells of that day, previous-ly foreign to my senses, are now frozen in my memory. I still hear police yelling out orders, horns honking, sirens blaring, high-pitched beeping coming from the firemen's equipment. A loud noise, a car backfiring, the smell of fire or of burning rubber or plastic — it doesn't take a lot to trigger my memory. To this day I think the strongest emotion that has remained with me is my own feeling of vulnerability.

Not long ago, I passed a man who was wearing a red necktie! I starred at his tie and paid a tribute to that poor man who had fallen through the air to his death. I spoke to him in my head. I said a silent prayer and told him, as I have done so often these post 9/11 years: 'I'm so sorry for the terror you experienced.' And then as always, I asked the man in the red tie to pray for us.

I'm sure that others who were affected by 9/11 have different memories and have learned different lessons. So many people were wounded or died, and so many still suffer. Things have changed. Many of the places I typically walked through in the course of my day before 9/11 - the shops and special people — no longer exist. But new places and new people and new memories are still emerging. We are carrying on, and I am forever grateful to be one of the lucky ones!

I can never forget the way complete strangers banded together and helped one another that day. Human beings are resilient and strong, and while we may not be as open and cooperative as we were right after the tragedy, strangers and friends and loved ones continue to work together in a new way. No matter what, we will always be New Yorkers!

JIM

"My father's death taught me how to live life full-throttle"

"Our hunger for meaning is never more urgent than during a crisis"

- Dr. Julius Segal

Growing Through Grief

"How has this bright, well-presented, eloquent man found his way to my therapy couch?" I thought, as I completed my initial interview with Jim, my new patient. He seemed, in the vernacular, to have it all. And the reality is, he did! As I told him in one of our early sessions: "You have all the furniture, Jim. We just need to rearrange it together."

At our first meeting, Jim said: "It's my wife who gets credit for suggesting I get help with these grief issues. I didn't realize just how badly I was doing until she brought it up. That's why I'm here, to sort it out."

Jim's father had recently lost a long battle with cancer, and Jim confessed he was still struggling. "I feel overwhelmed!" he said.

On one level, he was dealing with the business of his father's estate. As the eldest child, the role of family Patriarch was now placed squarely on his shoulders. Jim was not a man to shirk responsibility. Nor was he reluctant to assume the role. But, he was concerned about doing a good job and turning in a performance that would have pleased his father.

On a deeper level Jim was also struggling with his feelings about himself. He had a lot of responsibility, and he worried that resolving the legal and business concerns he'd inherited would overshadow dealing with the consuming and unpredictable emotion of his grief.

He admitted. "It's easier for me to handle the legal and financial aspects of Dad's death than managing all my emotions. In business, once you reach the bottom line, you can put it aside. With this emotional roller coaster, I can't seem to find the bottom line."

He lowered his head slightly, in a sign of discouragement: "I'm feeling fragmented and disorganized. I just want to regain some control in my life."

An intelligent and introspective man, Jim found himself pondering existential questions: *Who am I now? Was I a good son? As the eldest, what is my role in the family structure? When is it time to let go of my grief? My father cast a very large shadow; I wonder if I'll ever be able to fill my father's footprints?*

He held high standards of performance for himself, and he constantly worried that his grief and stress would interfere with his performance at work. Would he somehow be neglectful of the needs of his clients? In later meetings, he would look back at his concern and realize how much he had grown and evolved. He freely admitted that, as a result of his addressing and understanding his grief, he had become an even more insightful, empathetic and proficient professional.

Live Life Full Throttle

A profound, emotional and unexpected experience gave Jim the freedom to step out from under his father's shadow. "It was toward the end of summer, a few months after my Dad's death. I was driving along on a Detroit-area freeway after visiting my mother who was now very ill and in the hospital. I was on emotional overload then. I remember thinking: 'First Dad dies and now Mom's not doing well either. What's coming next?'

It was a sunny day," Jim recalled. "The sky was clear, cobalt blue. There was very little traffic, and it was quiet on the freeway. Suddenly a black motorcycle came roaring up from behind. The rider had an open lane to move on forward, but instead he zoomed in, slowed down to my speed, and rode evenly next to my front bumper," Jim gestured with his hands, demonstrating the positioning of his car and the motorcycle.

"I couldn't see his face," he continued, "only the back of him, his black helmet and his tee shirt. He stayed in sync with me, riding along beside me, long enough for me to read the words on the back of his shirt: 'LIVE

LIFE FULL THROTTLE.' Then, he roared away, down the freeway and out of sight."

"I was stunned!" he declared. "On that guy's shirt was my Dad's whole philosophy. He had always said it's important to live life full throttle! In my mind I could visualize my Dad doing something like that, taking the place of the faceless unknown rider, pulling up next to me just long enough to deliver his message, and speed off into the open road ahead."

Jim pondered the meaning of all this: "Was it coincidence? Perhaps 'a sign?' Maybe it was God? Maybe it was my Dad? I had no idea. All I knew was that it felt like a clear signal to me, a catalyst for action. I now realized I had permission to let-go, to persist through my struggles and somehow begin to 'live my own life full throttle.' It was an amazing experience!"

Adult Orphan

Jim's mother died almost a year after his Dad. Her death brought a different kind of grief. "When you lose both parents, you feel like an adult orphan," Jim said quietly. " There was something about losing my Mom that was quite different. The differences were clearly evident at each parents' memorial funeral service."

He compared the funerals: "Dad's service had a kind of positive energy, much like his attitude toward life. It was held outdoors on a gorgeous sunny day. Almost everyone spoke, sharing his or her own stories about Dad. A violinist played selections including 'Ode To Joy' befitting his generally upbeat personality."

"On the day of my mother's funeral it rained," Jim said. "Her service had a feeling of conservative tradition and propriety, even a bit of melancholy. We all held black umbrellas against the downpour, and listened to bagpipes playing 'Amazing Grace' — a reverent tribute to my Mom. It was sad and beautiful at the same time. Her funeral was just as it should have been."

Gradually, Jim continued to resolve his grief. He gained deeper understanding of his relationship with each parent, and became acquainted with his parents from a new perspective, a point of view that we all too often discover only after our parents die.

Over time, Jim also put to rest, his previous concern that his preoccupation with grief would hinder his work. In all reality, it was the opposite. In fact, he happily admitted that, by working through his own personal grief, he'd become even more empathetic and understanding in all of his professional and personal relationships.

One of the concluding aspects of his story is that, as Jim continued to move forward, he recognized the growth and insight he had experienced in his grief journey. He felt proud of the son he'd been to his parents, and he was pleased with the closeness and love he felt for his wife, two sons and his siblings.

Jim has experienced an exciting new sense of freedom. He no longer lives in his father's shadow. Today he lives comfortably with his own shadow.

KAY

"As a young widow, I grieved for myself and my broken-hearted teenage daughter, Shellee"

SISU — Perserverance

"There is a word in the Finnish culture, sisu," Kay explained. "Sisu means to endure adversity, to draw from something deep down inside you when you feel your strength fading. It's something you reserve for hard times." (Kay)

In Kay's Words

I was first initiated to the concept of sisu as a young widow of 39. My 15-year-old daughter, Shellee, and I were mourning the death of Jerry, my husband, and her father. The future looked bleak.

Today, as I tell my story, I feel strong and competent. Not only have I learned the meaning of sisu, I realize I've incorporated the concept of it into my life. When Jerry died my world turned upside down; and so did Shellee's. Since then, I've faced financial crisis and struggled with all the worries for my daughter that a single parent learns to understand.

Before these catastrophic events, my life was good. Jerry was a loving husband. My beautiful daughter Shellee, was just beginning to grab the brass ring of life. As a family, we were happy and busy. I'd gone back to college to further my education. Jerry took pride in good health, his career, and his active life style. He was a hockey-nut and he loved playing competitive hockey on a regular basis.

Then the bubble burst. It was in December of 1985, around the holidays. Jerry admitted he wasn't feeling well and reluctantly agreed to consult a doctor. We were stunned with the diagnosis! Pancreatic cancer. The doctor said he had "one to three weeks to live." What a shock!

Telling Shellee about Jerry's diagnosis was one of the hardest things I've ever had to do. "Oh no, not my Dad," she cried hysterically. Jerry was the fun paren, I was the disciplinarian.

During the course of Jerry's illness, my own Dad was dying of a rare form of liver cancer. Both Jerry and my Dad were in the same hospital, but on different floors. Dad's death, in 1986, was really difficult, but somehow I was prepared. You anticipate the death of an aging parent, but don't expect that your young, vital husband will die.

Jerry's doctors were amazed by his strength. They had predicted one to three weeks, and he lived almost a year and a half after his diagnosis. By the time of his death, Jerry had lost 100 pounds! How can I put into a few words what it was really like to watch my husband die? My mind protected me from the reality of the situation. In my denial, I kept thinking: "He looks the same, only thinner. He's just losing weight — not dying."

During his illness, although money was tight, we managed to take a few family trips. When Jerry died, I was grateful that we'd traveled and not just "saved for the future." That guilt would've been too much to bear.

When Jerry's condition deteriorated, he entered a hospice facility. The care there was excellent. We could come and go and his friends and his hockey team constantly visited, bringing tapes of their games. Early on in hospice care, team members arrived with six-packs of beer. When they were politely told beer was off limits, they switched to fudgesicles to keep Jerry supplied with treats.

Over the year and a half he was suffering, my heart ached for our daughter. Shellee was losing her Dad - the cool parent who biked and played hockey with her and who loved her without condition. I worried that I was so busy and preoccupied with being the grieving wife and care-giver, I was neglecting Shellee.

At that time I was working and going to college. I would leave work, go see Jerry, and come home exhausted. He'd call and beg me to return to hospice, and I would. I felt so sad, so cheated. I wanted to do something to ease his pain, but couldn't. Toward the end nothing helped. I even became angry with God. I gave up on God that year and for some years to follow.

Jerry died on a warm sunny day in April 1987.

Shortly before he died, I'd met with a funeral director because I needed to know what decisions to make and consider how I'd be able to handle the costs. Planning a funeral for my husband was an entirely new experience for me.

Prior to my appointment at the funeral home, I'd made up my mind that if I didn't like this man or the funeral home, I'd simply go some place else. However, he was very kind and immediately put me at ease. His name was Monty, and he walked me through the steps I'd need to take. He also made suggestions. He had unusual insight and practical ideas, and he gave me a feeling of security and control. Monty was the one to explain to me: "Your daughter's first ride in a limousine should be for her high school prom, not her Dad's funeral." I agreed with him, and at the funeral my cousin, Dan, drove us to the cemetery in our family car.

Shellee was included in all the funeral plans, and I was determined to make the decisions for Jerry's funeral using my heart and not my head. As I look back, they were good decisions. Jerry had lost so much weight he didn't look like himself at the end. I provided the funeral director with a photo showing Jerry prior to his illness, when he was happy and healthy. Then, with the funeral director's effort, we had an open casket. The first time Shellee saw her Dad in the casket, she said something so reflective of the love and humor she and I share:

"Gee, Mom, Dad looks better than you do!"

Before he died Jerry had given me instructions: "I want six pall bearers. Use our cousin Dan and five hockey friends, and have them positioned as they would be on the ice — right wing, left wing and such." Jerry got his six pallbearers and we buried him with his favorite hockey stick.

The minister who officiated at the funeral suggested we ask family and friends to write a personal note, an anecdote, story or message to share with everyone. He would read all the messages during the funeral. He wisely said: "Everyone has important memories to share, but sometimes people are reluctant to stand up and speak at a funeral. Then they regret it later. This way everyone has an opportunity to participate." I've always appreciated his suggestion!

Hundreds of relatives and friends came (including the 30 members of Jerry's hockey team). As funerals go, it was a very meaningful one. Following Jerry's instructions, his tombstone bears the quotation: "I fought the good fight."

Carrying on for my Daughter

When Jerry died I lost part of my heart. I knew I'd never be quite the same. But I also knew, while it wouldn't be easy, my daughter and I would be all right. I had to have the strength to go on for her. Money was tight and I was now the breadwinner. Shellee and I were eligible for food stamps, but didn't take them. I continued working and going to school and I encouraged Shellee to try hard to carry on also. We had to make it all work!

In the months that followed the funeral, Shellee and I each struggled differently with our grief. Finally I realized we needed help. Counseling was expensive and took more time and energy than I anticipated. I'd never been to therapy before. My expectations were that you go in, pay your money and the therapist "fixes you!" You're paying for it and they should "fix it" by giving you specific steps to feeling better. I wanted the therapist to do the work. I was a little surprised (and angry, too) to learn that my counselor was only a guide. I had to do the work! Looking back, my therapist really helped me move forward into the unknown. She also reassured me that the way I was feeling was normal. She helped me conquer my own fear, but even more, she helped me understand my daughter's grief.

I discovered that other people in your life are important, too. They can help, even though sometimes it feels that they're hindering. Some people say hurtful, insensitive things. I was surprised when a friend said: "Look at you! You're blond, young and pretty — you'll have no problems." I think many people just don't know what to say or do.

I was widowed before I was 40. There weren't many soul sisters who could relate to my loss. Some friends avoided me; as though widowhood was something "you could catch." The old friends who hung in with me were invaluable. They made me feel that I mattered, and we are all stronger for it. I also made a lot of new friends, who helped me create new memories and find fresh meaning and activity.

Dating? — "He's NOT my Jerry!"

I started dating as a step to regain my life. It wasn't always fun and it wasn't easy. People tried to fix me up, and I gave it a try. I felt awkward because I'd been out of the social loop for so long. Even deciding what to wear became a chore! The bed would be heaped with outfits before I picked one to wear on a date. I worried about crazy little things like: What should I talk about? What should I do with my food if I'm too nervous to eat? What if I make a complete fool of myself?

My first relationship was a disappointment. Everything that man did annoyed me. Looking back I realized he just wasn't "my Jerry." I wasn't really ready to make room for a new man in my life. I'd take my time.

At this point I knew, for Shellee's sake, I had to move on in my life. She and I were a team and I had to hold up my end. I kept telling myself: "Don't give up."

In my grief, I was discouraged and fearful, but I finally came to realize Jerry would always be part of my life. This realization gave me the permission to move on. For me, moving forward meant making changes including changing my friendships and activities, my job and even the furniture in my home. I focused on getting physically and emotionally stronger. For a brief time, I took antidepressants. It helped.

As time progressed I started remembering the good things about life. Since then I've overcome two battles with cancer. I've also met and married a wonderful man, and together we've enjoyed watching Shellee become an amazing young woman. Shellee is now a wife, a great pediatric oncology nurse and, of course, my wonderful daughter.

Through my experience I wanted to help other women who'd lost their husbands and I decided to put together **A Widow's Guide to Dating:**

- Give it a try! Go on every date, no matter what a moron he may be. You're bound to learn something about your date and about yourself.
- Be cautious about meeting strangers. Great dating sources are: friends-of-friends, your church or synagogue, and getting involved

with people you meet through a common interest, club, hobby or work. Use social networking and the Internet wisely!

- Don't worry about what to wear, what to say, or what to order at the restaurant. You may be too nervous to eat anyway. Wear what makes you comfortable, and just keep the conversation moving. You'll be fine!

- Don't drink too much. Two things can happen: You'll either babble about your dead spouse, or you might behave in a way you'll regret the next morning.

- Don't rush it. Go slowly and gently and take all the time you need. Don't "settle" just because you don't like living alone. Everything is a learning experience — the more you try the more you learn.

- Don't give up.

SHELLEE
"When my Dad died, I felt like I had to take care of my Mom and myself"

"I know how important grief is to our healing. It gives us life again"

- Shellee

My Dad died when I was 15. If you've read my Mom's story, in the preceding chapter, you'll see that my grief is quite different from my Mom's. We get along wonderfully now, but for a while we both had to struggle.

Now, a couple of decades later, I still cry when I think of all the things I've missed sharing with my Dad. He didn't see me graduate from high school or college, nor walk me down the aisle at my wedding. He and I were great buddies. He went from being a fun, strong, healthy, hands-on dad, building an ice skating rink in our backyard, to a man being consumed by cancer.

I was devastated when he died!

During Dad's illness I was bombarded by emotion. I was scared and angry, lonely and frustrated. I hated the word "cancer." My Grandpa, whom I call Poppa, had terminal liver cancer and now my Dad was dying of pancreatic cancer. Cancer was all around me, and who could help? I had no siblings, my friends were busy being teenagers and my Mom was absorbed in her own grief.

It seemed as though I was the ONLY one going through this and that no one could possibly understand. Questions kept spinning in my mind. *Why MY Dad? What caused his cancer? How bad was his pain? Why can't the doctors do more? What should I say to him? How will I ever get along without my best buddy? Mom's a mess. Will I have to take care of HER now? Why do I feel like I'm losing BOTH parents! I felt alone in the world!*

And then Dad died.

The days of the funeral kept us so busy, even though we had a lot of support. None of it seemed "real." Mom and I did our best to deal with the deluge of emotions we each were confronting. We were trying to live one day at a time, but it was hard for both of us. I did find one source of comfort. I would put on Dad's gold rope necklace and wrapped myself up in his huge hockey jersey. It smelled like him and when I wore it, I felt like his strong arms were around me, protecting me from the world.

Shortly after Dad's funeral, I was going to the prom with my new boyfriend. We'd met shortly before the first time my Dad went into the hospital. Mom and I were having a heated argument about what time I needed to be home from the prom. She'd shout: "You need to be home at 1:00 am!" I'd shout back: "No one has to be home at all!" The fight continued, and in the thick of it, something unusual happened. A small wreath on the wall, firmly affixed by a three-inch nail, suddenly flew off the wall. It brought us up short and we said at the same time: "Dad says 2:00 am. That's the time to come home." Since then, I've come to believe that the people who "pass" watch over us, and in moments like our prom argument, loved ones make it known that they are still there.

Now I am a Registered Nurse, specializing in oncology. I previously worked with hospice, and currently I work with children who have cancer. Remembering Dad's death, I truly felt that I'd run far away from anything to do with cancer. Instead, I find myself gravitating to it, and immersing myself in helping patients and families who are struggling with the disease. I'm drawn to those families who are experiencing the feelings I used to have. I want to be the nurse who answers all their questions. I want to be there for them when it's time for my patient to pass. Families have my cell number and can call me at anytime!

Taking time to listen to families tell stories about their loved one is important to me. I've learned so much from working with others and from my own experience. My work in pediatric oncology has shown me that children have amazingly keen insight and understanding. I encourage loved ones to talk honestly with their kids who are patients. I reassure them that at times it's all right to give their loved one permission to "give up the fight." Many dying patients find comfort and reassurance, knowing that you love them very much and that you'll be able to carry on after they die.

I still cry at funerals. My patients and their families quickly become parts of my own family. It's a struggle to not get so involved, but I know how important grief is to our healing. It gives us life again. I'm excited to think about the future that's waiting for me. I'm also hoping that perhaps one day we'll find a cure for cancer.

In my whole grief experience, there's one thing I remember most often. It's something my friend, Chuck, said to me. At the time, Chuck was a teenager, and his Dad had sadly died of a massive heart attack. He put it this way:

"Everyone you love in your life has a place in your heart. Then that person dies, and the pain you feel is beyond words. It leaves a huge, empty spot in your heart. As time goes by, you visit that empty spot less often and the pain decreases. That's when you start to remember the good times and you smile instead of cry when you visit those memories. You never forget the person — EVER! That person has your heart and will never leave, but you are free to move forward."

MARGARET
"I'M NOT SAD EARL'S GONE. I'M JUST HAPPY I HAD HIM SO LONG"

"Grow old along with me. The rest is yet to be.
The last of life, for which the first was made"

- Robert Browning

Earl's death was not a surprise to Margaret.

When you're an 89-year-old woman, death is familiar. I've been to many funerals of friends and relatives. And now, to my own husband's funeral. Earl died peacefully at home. He was 90. Fortunately, I was at home with him when he died. I see that as the ultimate gift. How can I complain about that?

Earl and I often talked, even joked, about the predictability of taxes and death. Earl called death "Mr. Death — the silent companion." We were pretty realistic about life and grateful we had lived so long. We lived life to the fullest. Most folks our ages and younger have lost someone to Mr. Death.

At 89 I think I'm pretty vital. I keep up with the world and read the daily papers. I admit sometimes I scan the obituaries. And, I feel so badly when I read of the death of a young person. My heart aches over the death of a child, a young or middle-aged person, or someone killed overseas in the military. When you are young and a life is cut short, I think grief is much worse.

How different that is from my experience! Earl and I had a wonderful and long time together.

In the papers when I read about grief support groups, I can see how those groups can help some people, especially the young folks. I admit I miss Earl every day, but I don't grieve for him. The way I feel is calm, peaceful and resigned.

When we married, Earl was 20 and I was 19. That gave us around 70 years together. Sure, we had our ups and downs. We didn't always get along perfectly, and that seems natural. Also, at times we struggled with health issues and lack of money. In those 70 years we also saw a lot of things happen in the world; some things amazing and some not so good.

But, looking at the overall picture, Earl and I did pretty darned well.

Our large garden out back was the glue that held us together. We started our garden out of necessity. Our budget was limited and we needed the food to can or freeze. But over the years, our garden grew from being a necessity to a passion. Each year, we worked together side-by-side, planting, harvesting, and canning or freezing our crops.

Even when we had a spat, we worked well together in the garden.

Mr. Death walks quietly with me. I'm in no hurry. I take each day as it comes along. I hope to see Earl again in Heaven, if things like that do happen. And if it doesn't happen that I meet him again; well, I have 70 years of memories and tenderness to carry me along.

I'm not sad because Earl is gone; I'm just very happy that I had him for so long.

CHAPTER SIX

Conclusion

MOVING FORWARD

"EVENTUALLY WE GAIN THE STRENGTH TO PICK
UP THE OARS AND MOVE FORWARD IN LIFE"

"*I do not believe that sheer suffering teaches. If suffering alone taught, all the world would be wise, since everyone suffers. To suffering must be added mourning, understanding, patience, love, openness, and the willingness to remain vulnerable. All these and other factors combined, if the circumstances are right, can teach and can lead to rebirth*"

- Anne Morrow Lindbergh

Moving Forward

It's sad, but a reality. Grief and loss are confusing, disheartening life experiences. The unfortunate thing is that, as a society, we are just beginning to understand the emotional roller coaster that can begin with personal loss. We often seem to give in to the feeling that loss can be "dealt with" in a prescribed time and manner, and it's difficult to accept the reality that "mourning" lasts longer and can be more painful than most of us ever anticipated.

Getting through grief takes time. And it doesn't matter whether the death is sudden or anticipated. These emotions are part of the "healing process," and each person embarks on this self-discovery path at his or her personal pace. When we are in the middle of the roller coaster of grief, it is difficult to acknowledge that there can be comforting aspects of this journey. But we must remember that the most important first step is to give ourselves permission to grieve.

One of my most rewarding life lessons came from my sister, Sally. She introduced me to the infinite opportunities for love and closeness that approaching death often offers. Sally taught me how to capture life's golden moments and to capitalize on that precious, non-negotiable element we call "time."

Be aware, special opportunities for understanding and love often arise out of the grieving period and they become integral parts of our new story, as we carry these past memories into the future.

Although the journey through grief can be lonely, discouraging, and often baffling, there are several important "Rules of the Road" I'd like to share with you.

If we love someone and we lose that person — we will grieve.

Grieving is a normal, natural response to loss.

Grief, while a simple concept, is a complicated process.

It takes place over time, which is difficult to measure.

Grief, which has many faces, is a very personal journey.

It's sad but true. We often get worse before we get better.

Grief is actually a testimony to our ability to love others.

Memory is the cradle of love, helping us toward resolution of our loss.

It is possible to move ahead, finding new direction and recognizing vital, new energy.

Resolving loss and grief provides each of us with the meaningful opportunity to once again fully appreciate life.

Grief can become our cornerstone to personal growth.

Who Can I Call?

Resources for Loss and Bereavement, Trauma and Chronic Illness

"The pain of bereavement seems to leave fewer scars
when shared than when it is borne alone"
- Dr. Julius Segal

There are community-wide resources which can help families, friends and neighbors who may need assistance with particular issues. The following list offers information, guidance, and support. This list is drawn from national, state, and local resources and is arranged in alphabetical order. Please note that contact numbers and web addresses change over time, and you may find it helpful to consult an Internet source for current information.

Alzheimers Association is an alliance of professionals and family members dedicated to helping patients with Alzheimer's Disease and their families. The Association also provides education, information, advocacy, and support.

 1.800.272.3900

 225 N Michigan Ave / Fl 17 / Chicago, IL / 60601-7633

 www.alz.org

American Cancer Society (ACS) addresses many forms of cancer, and provides information, resources, treatment protocols, and support information for patients, caregivers and families, including children. ACS can also direct callers to local contact sources.

 1.800.227.2345

 250 Williams Street, NW / Atlanta, GA / 30303

 www.cancer.org

American Red Cross is a worldwide organization which provides supportive services for: educational programs, national and international disaster relief programs, military members and their families, community services for the homeless and unemployed, abandoned children, and blood donor resources.

 1.800.RED.CROSS (733.2767)

 2025 E Street, NW / Washington, DC / 20006

 www.redcross.org

American Self-Help Clearinghouse is a first-step internet resource for locating many types of available national, international, and on-line self-help groups. The Clearinghouse also offers *The Self-Help Sourcebook*, a book full of helpful information and guides.

 1.973.989.1122

 375 E McFarlan St / Dover, NJ / 07801

 www.mentalhelp.net/selfhelp/

Amyotrophic Lateral Sclerosis (ALS) is also known as Lou Gehrig's Disease. This name came from the baseball player, Lou Gehrig, who died of ALS. The ALS Association National Office maintains a telephone and referral service dedicated to family caregiver support, patient assistance resources, insurance questions and medical products. It is also a referral service for locating local area ALS chapters.

 1.800.782.4747

 27001 Agoura Rd / Suite 250 / Calabasas Hills, CA / 91301

 www.alsa.org

<u>Association for Death Education & Counseling (ADEC)</u> a group of educators and clinicians, formed in 1976, is the oldest interdisciplinary organization in the field of death, dying, and grief. ADEC provides caregiver information, referrals to therapists specializing in death and dying, grief counseling, grief resources, group meetings, and information.

 1.847.509.0403

 111 Deer Lake Rd / Suite 100 / Deerfield, IL / 60015

 www.adec.org

<u>Center for Disease Control (CDC)</u> provides information on treatment options and referral for personal issues on matters related to HIV-AIDS, Sexually Transmitted Diseases (STD's), Tuberculosis (TB), and viral hepatitis.

 1.800.CDC.INFO (232.4636)

 1600 Clifton Rd / Atlanta, GA / 30333

 www.cdc.gov

The Centering Corporation provides education and referrals to reading materials, and a wide variety of resources and brochures on grief and loss for professionals and families in grief, including information for the people confronting the sudden, traumatic death of a loved one.

 1.866.218.0101

 7230 Maple St / Omaha, NE / 68134

 www.centering.org

Compassionate Friends is a national bereaved parents organization which provides information on the death of children, grief and bereavement guides, written and video materials, and referrals to local self-help meetings. Compassionate Friends holds bereaved parent support group meetings throughout the nation, and provides information on state and local chapters.

 1.877.969.0010

 900 Jorie Blvd / Suite 78 / Oak Brook, IL / 60523

 www.compassionatefriends.org

GriefNet provides internet resources offering assistance with a wide range of issues for adults, children, and teens. The website provides varied resources, information, guidance to support groups, and interaction with other professionals in the area of death and dying. Specific topics covered include: losses that are sudden and losses that are anticipated, loss of a child, loss of a parent, loss of a spouse or partner, children in grief, loss of a sibling or friend, losses related to health issues and war and combat losses. GriefNet also provides a kid-friendly website, www.kidsaid.com, for children and teens. "Kids Aid" is a safe place for children to share with one another and for parents and kids to ask questions and find answers. It is supervised by Cendra Lynn, Ph.D.

 1.734.761.1960

 P.O. Box 3272 / Ann Arbor, MI / 48106-3272

 www.griefnet.org / www.kidsaid.com

International Association of Trauma Professionals (IATP) is an organization designed to unite trauma counselors. IATP provides awareness of the effects of trauma, establishes standards of competency for those counseling survivors of trauma and offers personal support for caregivers in the field of trauma and intervention.

 Not available

 5104 N Lockwood Ridge Rd / Suite 303E / Sarasota FL / 34234

 www.traumaprofessional.net

Mental Health Net is an internet resource providing comprehensive information via weblinks, which focus on mental and physical health, and concerns regarding assistance with illness and treatment. Among the areas covered are: child and adolescent problems, depression, stress management, sexual dysfunction, personality disorders, articles pertinent to mental and physical health, and assistance finding therapists in local areas.

 Not available

 Not available

 www.mentalhelp.net/

The National AIDS Hotline provides information and support pertaining to AIDS, and can be contacted through the Center for Disease Control.

 1.800.448.0440

 1600 Clifton Road NE / Atlanta, GA / 30333

 www.cdc.gov/hiv

National Funeral Directors Association (NFDA) provides verbal and written resources on funerals, memorial services, burial and cremation, and other bereavement issues, including referrals to local and state-wide affiliates.

 1.800.228.6332

 13625 Bishop Drive / Brookfield, WI / 53005

 www.nfda.org

National Hospice and Palliative Care Organization is dedicated to maintaining quality care for terminally ill persons and their families. The NHPCO provides education, professional resources, and support for hospice patients and their loved ones.

 1.800.658.8898 / 1.800.646.6460

 1731 King Street / Suite 100 / Alexandria, VA / 22314

 www.nhpco.org

The National Institute for Trauma and Loss in Children (TLC) provides resources for caregivers, including guidelines for practitioners and those enduring trauma. They also offer trauma intervention programs, training assemblies, and in-depth workshops for professionals.

 1.800.315.8640

 42855 Garfield Road / Suite 111 / Clinton Township, MI / 48038

 www.starrtraining.org

<u>The National Suicide Prevention Lifeline</u> is available to assist individuals who are facing trauma, suicide or emotional crisis, and offers materials, lists of warning signs, crisis center locations, and contact information. This organization provides support, information, and links to community resources, helping individuals locate the nearest available suicide prevention center and mental health provider.

 1.800.SUICIDE (784-2433) / 1.800.273.TALK (8255)

 Not available

 suicidepreventionlifeline.org

<u>Parents of Murdered Children (POMC)</u> is a national organization designed for parents, families, and other victims of homicide. POMC provides legal information, lists of local advocacy self-help groups, and interaction with the criminal justice system. POMC also provides on-going emotional support with the acute grief issues resulting from traumatic loss and helps parents and other survivors resolve their personal grief.

 1.888.818.7662

 100 East 8th Street / Suite 202 / Cincinnati, OH / 45202

 www.pomc.com

Sudden Infant Death Syndrome (SIDS) offers assistance to families and professionals dealing with SIDS, including hope, help, healing, support, and resources listed by state. The center also tries to connect individuals to programs, services, and information related to infant death by SIDS.

 1.800.421.3511

 1120 South 6th Street / Suite 100 / St. Louis, MO / 63104

 www.sidsresources.org

Survivors of Homicide is a national organization offering support to those coping with the murder of a loved one. They provide local support groups which deal with survivors of a homicide, and provides information about the criminal justice system, and how to identify advocacy programs for victims of violent crime.

 1.888.833.4764

 530 Silas Deane / Suite 380 / Weathersfield, CT / 06109

 www.survivorsofhomicide.com

<u>Tragedy Assistance Program for Survivors (TAPS)</u> offers tragedy assistance resources for anyone suffering the loss of a loved one serving in the military. TAPS is available 24/7, providing comfort, peer-based emotional support, casework assistance, crisis intervention, good-grief camps, survivor seminars, and grief and trauma printed and video material.

 1.800.959.8277

 1777 F Street, NW / 6th Floor / Washington, DC / 20006

 www.taps.org

<u>Veteran Affairs (VA)</u> provides a wide range of services and assistance to veterans and families. Their concern is the physical and mental well-being of the veteran. In addition to mental and physical issues, the VA provides benefits, insurance, death benefits, counseling and support. The organization has a confidential life chat service (chat with a live counselor) which is available 24 hours/day, 7 days/week.

 1.800.827.1000

 810 Vermont Avenue Northwest / Washington, DC / 20420

 www.veteranscrisisline.net / www.va.gov

Widowed Persons Service (WPS) was established in 1973. WPS is comprised of men and women of all backgrounds and ages who are seeking guidance and support in dealing with the death of a spouse. The national organization provides information on local chapters, outreach, telephone service, public education, mutual self-help groups, and a referral service. WPS offers training for outreach volunteers wishing to organize support groups and counseling for other widowed persons.

 1.817.293.4749

 2906 SE Loop 820 / Suite A / Ft Worth, TX / 76140

 www.wpstc.org

Wounded Warrior Project (WWP) provides programs and services for injured members of the military, during the period between active duty and the transition back to civilian life. The mission of this organization is to "honor and empower wounded warriors."

 1.877.832.6997

 4899 Belfort Road / Suite 300 / Jacksonville, FL / 32256

 www.woundedwarriorproject.org

Young Widow provides an interactive website, available to young men and women dealing with the death of a spouse. The site is dedicated to helping them to "recover, reclaim, and rebuild." Their forum style young window bulletin board is always available for contacting others online who can offer friendship, support, and encouragement. This site offers reviews of pertinent books, resources on living alone, and information about local support groups for kids and teens.

 Not Available

 P.O. Box 902 / Mount Kisco, NY / 10549

 www.youngwidow.org

Credits

Marilyn Kuperus Gilbert (Chapter, Cover Photographer)

Michael Dean Gilbert (Illustrator)

Stephanie Lindberg (Graphic Designer)

John T. Lynch, Ph.D. (Consultant)

Carl M. Karoub, MD (Consultant)

Lori McCracken (Biography Photographer)

Norman J. Menton, MD (Consultant)

Annie Moldafsky, The Moldafsky Group (Editor)

Jean Peterson (Chapter Photographer)

Van Shipley (Publisher)

Reverend Thomas Slowinski (Consultant)

Kay L. Sturgeon (Consultant)

References

William Bridges, <u>Transitions</u>

Robert Browning, "Along The Road"

Dwight David Eisenhower

Viktor Frankl, MD

Rabbi Earl Grollman

Carl M. Karoub, MD

HBO - Television Series, *Six Feet Under*

Elisabeth Kubler-Ross, MD

Ambassador Bruce Laingen

Anne Morrow Lindbergh, <u>Hour of Gold, Hour of Lead</u>

Henry W. Longfellow, "The Children's Hour"

William Manchester, <u>Goodbye Darkness</u>

Doug Manning, <u>Don't Take My Grief Away From Me</u>

Beryl Markum, <u>West With the Wind</u>

Andrew Marvell, "To His Coy Mistress"

Norman J. Menton, MD, "Sally"

Julius Segal, Ph.D., <u>Winning Life's Toughest Battles</u>

Reverend Thomas Slowinski

Rabindranath Tagore, <u>Fireflies</u>

The Talmud

CPSIA information can be obtained at www.ICGtesting.com
Printed in the USA
BVOW011257310812

299275BV00001B/4/P